Effective Business Writing

Effective Business Writing

STRATEGIES AND SUGGESTIONS

Maryann V. Piotrowski

PERENNIAL LIBRARY

HARPER & ROW, PUBLISHERS, New York
Grand Rapids, Philadelphia, St. Louis, San Francisco
London, Singapore, Sydney, Tokyo, Toronto

First PERENNIAL LIBRARY edition published 1990.

Library of Congress Cataloging-in-Publication Data

Piotrowski, Maryann V.
    [Re : writing]
  Effective business writing : strategies and suggestions / Maryann V. Piotrowski.
    p. cm.
  Reprint. Originally published: Re : writing. New York : Harper & Row, c1989.
  Includes bibliographical references.
  ISBN 0-06-091972-8
  1. Business writing. I. Title.
[HF5718.3.P56 1990]
808'.066651—dc20
                       89-46220

90 91 92 93 94 CC/FG 10 9 8 7 6 5 4 3 2 1

*To the memory of my father,
and to my mother and brother*

Contents

Acknowledgments

Writing is a lonely activity. I was never truly alone, however. My family and friends were always there for me—encouraging and cheering me on. They were also patient. When they asked, "How is the book coming along?" they listened politely as I described—sometimes at great length—the book's progress. I wish to thank them all.

Special thanks to Barbara Swartz, Anne McDonald, Lee Warren, Jennifer Presley, Sandy Nickel, Dan Daniels, and Jennifer Mapes, who read and reacted to sections of the book. Special thanks also to Roger Richards, who read the book at every stage of its progress. His sound advice and quick wit helped me write, revise, and retain my good humor. Thanks also to Loretta Caira, the fastest typist in all New England.

Finally, I'd like to thank William Zinsser for his interest and encouragement and Buz Wyeth, executive editor of Harper & Row, for his support and suggestions.

Preface

If you were asked what job-related tasks you most dislike, would "writing" be on your list? If so, you are not unusual. Many others who work in industry, the public sector, and the professions openly admit to a dislike of writing. Besides "hating" writing—to use the word they use—these writers say they spend too much time writing, and, when they finally send out a document, neither they, their bosses, nor their readers find it effective.

Yet you, like others, realize that the ability to write well is an important skill—and one that brings you great visibility. Just as you judge others by their writing, so too others judge you by your writing. The memos, letters, and reports you write provide powerful evidence of your overall competence and of your management style.

This book can help you improve your writing. It focuses on issues many business writers find troublesome. You can read this book from cover to cover or you can use it as a reference book; it is organized so that you can easily look up specific topics.

This book is a distillation of what I've learned about business writing from several different perspectives: as a junior executive in banking and finance; as a writing instructor at Harvard Business School and at Massachusetts Institute of Technology's Sloan School of Management; as a writer and editor of the newsletter *Re: Writing,* from which this book evolved; and as a communication consultant to such clients as Time, Inc., Manufacturers Hanover Trust Company, General Cinema, Dupont NEN Products, and the U.S. Civil Service Commission, among others.

I hope that this book will help you become a more competent and more confident writer.

—MARYANN V. PIOTROWSKI
Cambridge, Massachusetts

Effective Business Writing

Bad Writing Is Bad for Business

Efficiently run businesses cannot tolerate inefficient memos, letters, and reports. Business stops, or is slowed, as a result of poor communication. Orders don't get delivered or they don't get delivered on time; tasks don't get done, or they don't get done correctly. Productivity decreases while labor and supervisory costs increase. The morale of employees suffers, as does the image of the firm.

William J. Gallagher, who was for many years Manager of Communication Services at Arthur D. Little, Inc., has estimated that up to 30 percent of letters and memos in industry and government do nothing more than seek clarification of earlier correspondence or respond to that request for clarification. That estimate does not include the thousands of letters and memos that are not acted upon because they are not understood. Bad writing is bad for business.

Most people in business—employers and employees alike—agree that writing skills are weak. Some of the causes for poor writing clearly stem from a lack of instruction, or poor instruction, in our schools. But many of the causes have little to do with schooling iself; rather, they emanate from attitudes held by the writers themselves or from limitations prevalent in the workplace.

Some Causes of Poor Writing

One or more of the following causes may contribute to poor writing:

Ignoring the reader. Readers today want as much information as possible in as little time as possible. They want to know instantly what a piece of writing is about, and they want to understand it after one careful but quick reading. Writers who ignore their readers, sometimes quite unconsciously, do so by giving too much, too little, or the wrong kind of information. They use specialized vocabulary; their style is dense or bureaucratic.

A lack of professional pride. Some writers do not consider writing to be a part of their professional duties; therefore, they are unwilling to give it the time and discipline it requires. They are bankers, chemists, accountants, or marketing managers— not writers. Writing is a nuisance to them.

A lack of confidence. Some writers lack confidence in their ability to write so they rely on the file cabinet to do their writing. They find several letters in the files and by borrowing paragraphs, moving around sentences, and changing words, they put together a "new" letter, but one that is, nonetheless, unclear.

Inexperience. Since much business is conducted over the phone, at meetings, and in casual conversations, some writers lack experience. Even though they may have learned basic writing skills in school, they have not had sufficient exposure to, or practice in, writing for business. The style of academic writing is quite different from that of business writing.

Writing for the wrong reason. Some writers write to impress others, not to express themselves. They think that they will not appear educated or knowledgeable unless they dip every word in gold, unless they embroider every sentence. Some of these writers are simply insecure. They camouflage their ideas lest they be attacked. Others are unseasoned. They do not yet realize that top executives do not need to adopt airs.

Strict requirements. Some writers do not write well because their bosses set strict requirements. One boss may demand what he or she is used to: "That's the way we've done it for years." Another may set limits: "I won't read anything over a page long." If it were not for these requirements, the written product could be far better.

Understanding the causes may help both employees and their employers identify the factors that may be contributing to bad business writing. Once the causes have been identified, remedies may suggest themselves.

Writing Is an Essential Skill

In many cases, doing business today demands that employees routinely learn new skills. When there are so many new skills to learn, is it really so important to master such a basic skill as writing? Yes, it is. The ability to write well is—and will continue to be—an essential business skill, especially in the new information society.

In their book *Re-Inventing the Corporation,* John Naisbett and Patricia Aburdene submit that "the more information we have, the more we need to be competent thinkers." Hand in hand with the ability to think is the ability to write. While men and women in business must keep up with the times and learn the many new skills that will give them access to greater information, they must also master the skills that will enable them to use and communicate this information. In fact, Naisbett and

Aburdene, among others, foresee a revival in writing instruction.

At the same time that many graduate business schools began requiring students to take computer courses, they also began requiring students to take courses in written and oral communication. Today the top-tier business schools—at Harvard, Stanford, Dartmouth, Massachusetts Institute of Technology, New York University, Carnegie-Mellon, Cornell, and The University of Pennsylvania, among others—include communication courses in their curricula. Managing well means communicating well.

Writing is an important skill on the job and in life. As William Zinsser, writer, editor, and teacher points out in his book *Writing to Learn,* "Far too many Americans are prevented from doing useful work because they have never learned to express themselves. Contrary to general belief, writing is not something that only 'writers' do; writing is a basic skill for getting through life."

The workplace is very much a part of life, and writing is very much a part of the workplace. The ability to write well—clearly, concisely, and precisely—should not be considered an ancillary skill; it should be considered an essential skill. Good writing is good for business.

2

Getting Started

Gaining Control

When a writing deadline approaches, or when a client or superior says, "Get it to me by tomorrow," you simply must get started. First you have to gain control of yourself. Then you have to gain control of your topic.

Gaining control of yourself requires that you put your mind and energy to the task. You may have to subdue the panic that the time pressure and the difficulty of the task impose, or you may have to circumvent your own clever procrastination rituals.

Getting started might mean that you need to think more, or it might mean that you need only close the door, have your calls answered, and begin writing. Whatever it takes to discipline yourself, do it.

You'll also have to gain control of your ego. You may come to a subject with knowledge and opinions that differ from those of your reader, yet egocentrism may keep you from seriously considering the other person's point of view. Being aware of your reader's perspective will help you avoid false starts.

Gaining control of your topic means nothing more than

defining the task. Until you know what you have to do, you cannot begin doing it. The following methodical approach might help you overcome inertia and focus on the task. Ask yourself these questions:

PURPOSE: Am I writing to inquire, inform, persuade, motivate, or do I have more than one purpose?

Besides writing to convey my thoughts, do I have some personal or political agenda? To go on record? To protect myself? To gain visibility?

SCOPE: Given my needs and my readers' needs, how much information should I include?

CONTENTS: What kinds of information will help me achieve my purpose?

Do I have all the information I need?

How, or where, can I get additional information?

CONSTRAINTS: What can work against me, or make my task more difficult? Time or cost constraints? My reader's attitudes? My own lack of credibility?

By answering questions like these, your task will become less amorphous, more concrete. As you gain control and get involved in the task, your lethargy will fade and your energy will build.

Seeing the Message Through Your Reader's Eyes

Put yourself in your reader's place and look at the world, and your message, through that person's eyes. This simple technique can help you get started on a project and, ultimately, write a document that is effective.

If your boss's desk is piled high with papers because it's a busy time of year, you may want to think twice about sending a long memo that may not get read, however important the matter is to you. Instead, send a short one that gives the essentials—no more. If a customer points out that he is having trouble comparing and deciding upon one of several plans your company offers, write a simple follow-up letter comparing the plans for him.

If you do not give your readers the amount and kinds of information they need, if you do not write at their level of understanding, if you do not respond to their mood, your message may be ignored—or you may have to write yet another memo or letter on the same topic.

Before you write, ask yourself these questions about your reader:

How interested or involved in the subject is my reader?
How knowledgeable is he or she about the subject?
What is my reader's purpose for reading? To make a decision? To be better informed?
Does my reader have special concerns or strong views about the subject? What are they?
How does my reader regard me personally and professionally?
What is my reader's style of doing business?

Answering these questions will help you decide on the length, scope, content, structure, development, style, and tone of your message.

All readers are motivated by their needs and interests. If you can see your message through your reader's eyes, your task will be enormously simplified.

Writing for a Diverse Audience

Analyzing the needs of your reader is a primary step in planning an effective piece of writing. When you write to multiple readers who have a similar knowledge of and interest in the subject, you can write to one representative person in the audience. But when the intended readers have different needs, interests, or roles, your job is not so simple. How can you effectively reach a diverse audience?

Begin by identifying the primary readers and the secondary readers. Primary readers are those who have the greatest "need to know." They are the ones who will generally have to act, or reach some decision, after reading your report; thus, they are the ones you should cater to. Secondary readers are those who, while interested, do not need the same level of detail. They are generally reading to become informed, not to act. Resist the urge to cater to the secondary audience, even if they are of higher rank.

The following devices will help both sets of readers:

Covering memos. Write different covering memos to each audience. Primary readers will need little information in this memo, though you can use it to point them to sections of special interest to them. Secondary readers will appreciate all the guidance you can give them. Provide them with additional background or with supplementary information. Steer them toward sections of particular interest and away from sections that are too detailed or technical. Make them feel comfortable with the subject. If necessary, use this memo to deal with politically sensitive matters as well.

Summaries. Start with a summary of the whole report. If the report is long, also include internal summaries, either at the beginning or at the end of each section, so that both sets of readers will stay on track. Even if you must lapse into technical language elsewhere, keep the language in these summaries easy to understand. Secondary readers may not need to read anything more than the summaries.

Headings. Since not everybody will want to read everything, use lots of headings and subheadings. These will enable readers to find relevant information and skip over irrelevant information.

Marginal notations. Unless a document is highly formal, individualize it by adding customized comments in the margins. Use colored ink, Post-it notes, stars, or other symbols that will help readers.

Appendices. If you are including information of interest only to specialists, put it at the end of the report. The general reader will appreciate not having to wade through it, and the specialist will appreciate having it all together in one place.

Finally, realize that sometimes in trying to please everyone with one report, you may please no one. If the needs of the audiences are so diverse that even the preceding suggestions will not help, write separate reports.

Organizing Your Thoughts

Once you've defined the purpose and scope of your document and have pulled together the information your reader needs, you may be tempted to begin writing at once. Resist the temptation.

Instead, sit back and ask yourself how you should organize the information for maximum clarity and impact. Avoid organizing the information the same way in which you thought it through. Most readers want the results of your thinking, not the thinking itself. Be ready to abandon traditional academic, scientific, or business patterns that require you to build to a conclusion. Most readers want to get important information at once.

Start by listing randomly all the ideas you want to include. Organizing from this list will help you see how the parts fit together. It will also help you experiment with various ways to organize the information. Organizing requires that you *choose* a structure, rather than merely settle for one.

Two factors should guide you in making this choice: the information and your reader.

The information. In most cases, the information itself will suggest an organizational pattern. For example, if your purpose were to describe a new procedure to your staff, the information—the steps in the procedure—would require that you organize the memo in strict chronological order. Similarly, if you were comparing the strengths and weaknesses of three job applicants in a memo to senior management, the memo would be organized around the information—a discussion of applicants A, B, and C.

Sometimes the information can be organized in more than one way. If you were explaining a decline in sales, for example, the causes for the decline might be related or unrelated. If they were related, you would show the causal relationship in the way you ordered the ideas (Reason A caused Reason B, which, in turn, caused Reason C). If the factors were unrelated, you would explain each cause separately, proceeding from the least important cause to most important, or vice versa. (In general, it is best to move from most important to least important information.) In each of these cases, you would have to make some decisions about the organization, though they would be few.

Your reader. Besides considering the information, you will have to consider your reader. Here, you will have to make more, and possibly more difficult, decisions. Your reader's familiarity with a subject and willingness to accept your point of view will guide you.

Assume, for example, that you are recommending to management that greater safety precautions be taken in a plant because four accidents occurred in the past year. If your readers knew about the accidents and were, you thought, receptive to your idea, you could begin by making your recommendation, reminding them of the accidents, underscoring the importance of the situation, and finally delineating the precautions you suggest. But if you knew that for one reason or another they were not receptive to your plan, you might begin by discussing the accidents and underscoring the importance of the situation, and only then making your recommendation. Finally, you might show how the precautions you suggest would prevent further accidents from occurring.

If your readers were unfamiliar with the situation, and thus had no opinion one way or the other, you might start by briefly describing the accidents and making your recommendation. (Both points could be covered in your opening paragraph.) You would then have to discuss the accidents in some detail and show how the precautions you recommend would prevent further accidents.

In each of the situations above, you would also have to decide on the order in which to describe the accidents. You could arrange them in one of three ways: by the order in which they occurred, by the degree of their seriousness, or by their causes.

The examples described above do not represent all the possible decisions you will have to make in organizing a piece of writing. But they do show that organizing your writing means making choices.

Trust yourself to make the right choice but only after you have taken the time to analyze both the information and your reader. The way a document is organized can make your writing easy or difficult to follow; it can increase or decrease your reader's receptivity to your message.

(Also see "Conclusions—First or Last?" on page 22.)

Finding an Efficient Writing System

Many writing projects take longer than they should simply because the writer hasn't thought about ways to do them more efficiently. Because writing is a creative process, it cannot be fully systematized. You cannot expect to turn out one memo after another with the same speed, precision, and degree of excellence. But by systematizing the writing process as much as possible, you may be able to produce routine correspondence in a predictable amount of time—an important consideration in most business situations.

Writing systems vary from writer to writer. Even the same writer may vary the system used according to his or her expertise on a subject, the kind of writing being done, its importance, or its reader. If you have a system that works for you, think of ways you can further streamline it. If you do not have a system, try using the one that follows. Going through these steps may help you be a more efficient writer:

Worrying and procrastinating
Deciding what to say
Organizing
Writing the draft
Getting distance from the draft
Revising the draft

Worrying and procrastinating may come quite naturally to you. Do not scold yourself for delaying a project at its outset, though, because you need some time to warm up to the topic, some time to let your mind wander, some time to let your ideas incubate. Many of your best ideas may, in fact, occur to you at odd moments during the day or night. Like many other writers, you may excel at this phase of the process but lack momentum to proceed to the next phases. Try setting a strict time limit for this step. Then mentally let go of the project. Allow your subconscious to take over—but only for the specified period of time.

Deciding what to say will be easier if you first put down all your ideas about a topic without evaluating or censoring them. Then select those ideas that are essential to your message and to your reader. Do not hesitate to throw away marginal ideas, for selectivity is important to good writing. If you have trouble coming up with enough ideas, or the right ones, you might need to do further reading. Sometimes talking to someone who is knowledgeable about the topic can help stimulate your thinking.

Organizing requires that you experiment with various approaches until you find one that does justice to the content, one that is easy to follow, and one that will keep your readers interested. Be careful that you do not simply replicate in the document the thought process you used in developing your ideas. You may, for example, have generated conclusions and recommendations only at the end of a complex reasoning process. Withholding these key ideas until the end of your document, however, might not serve the readers' interest. They might well want to know the results of your thinking immediately.

Writing the draft should be a quick, continuous process. Try to complete the draft in one sitting. Expect it to be rough. Many writers tend to overwork their writing at this stage. As a result, they get stuck or discouraged and toss the draft aside. If you find yourself getting bogged down, push on. Coming back to an imperfect draft is far better than coming back to an incomplete one.

Getting distance from the draft will allow you to see your work more objectively. Horace, the early Roman poet, is said to have suggested that no document be published for eight years after being written. This cooling-off period would allow the author to decide if a piece of writing were still worth publishing. Although Horace's timetable is poorly adapted to today's fast-paced world, his basic point is sound. If you can get away from your draft for eight days, eight hours, or even eight minutes, when you come back to it, you will readily notice ideas that should be added, omitted, or clarified.

Revising the draft may take as much as half your total writing time. In this phase, you'll test the ideas and structure of the document, rearrange sentences within paragraphs, rewrite awkward passages, choose words for precision and proper tone, and check the grammar and mechanics. This polishing stage will ensure that your writing is as professional as you are.

This system works for many writers, but you need not follow it slavishly. For example, you may be drafting a letter and choose to revise a poorly phrased sentence immediately, or you may be revising the draft and only then realize that you have omitted important facts. Every creative process requires flexibility. Do not let good ideas get away from you.

Clear writing demands clear thinking, which is itself a time-consuming process. You'll be more efficient once you have found a system that works for you. You'll fall into the rhythm of work, and your mood and the product will benefit.

Overcoming Writer's Block

Every writer has suffered at one time or another from writer's block—that painful inability to get one's thoughts on paper. This disability afflicts all kinds of writers: writers of fiction and of nonfiction, the disciplined and the undisciplined, the veteran and the novice. Unlike other maladies, writer's block is not cured by taking two aspirin and going to bed. On the contrary, such treatment aggravates the condition, since pressure mounts and panic increases as the task is delayed. Because each bout of writer's block may stem from a different cause, different treatments may be advisable.

Common Causes and Recommended Treatments

LACK OF PREPARATION

Frequently your ideas won't flow because you haven't decided what you want to say. Figuring out what you want to say while trying to say it may seem efficient, but this approach is counterproductive. You'll end up not thinking coherently and not communicating clearly.

Treatment: Before you begin to write you should be able to state what you hope to achieve and how you will go about achieving it. Don't begin writing unless you can say something like this: "I will recommend hiring two more editors and will support the recommendation by reviewing the importance of the editorial function, by comparing the size of our staff with that of other consulting companies, and by describing the backlog in the Publications Department."

MISCONCEPTIONS ABOUT WRITING

You might think that once prepared, you should be able to produce a nearly perfect product easily and swiftly.

Treatment: Recognize that writing is hard work. Although preparation will help, it will not eliminate the tedium of putting your thoughts into words. Even professional writers grope for their thoughts much the way one gropes for familiar objects in the dark.

SELF-CONSCIOUSNESS

Because your writing will be reviewed and criticized by others, you may become obsessed by what others will think of you.

Treatment: Careful preparation will help you decide what to say and will give you confidence that what you put on paper will not make you look foolish. Others are probably not nearly so critical as you imagine. They will quickly read what you have written, giving you the benefit of the doubt as to what you say and how you say it. (We all know of exceptions, of course.)

CONFUSING WRITING WITH EDITING

You may become bogged down because you edit excessively as you compose. Switching back and forth between creative and censoring modes interferes with the flow of ideas, words, and sentences.

Treatment: Separate the writing phase from the editing phase. When drafting your message write with no interruption. If you cannot think of the right words, capture your idea in words that come to you quickly. Your goal should be to get your ideas down, lest they escape you. Suspend criticism until you have completed the draft. Then apply your finest critical skills in evaluating and revising your writing.

BOREDOM

Working on a project often requires long hours of intensive reading, research, and discussion. It is not uncommon to reach a saturation point even before you begin writing.

Treatment: When possible, start each writing project far enough ahead of the deadline so that you can get away from the project when you begin to feel bored. Focus on the finished product and its importance to its readers. Allow the pride of authorship to override your boredom.

Additional Aids

1. Warm up to your subject by talking about it. Talk to a person or into a machine. Speaking is easier and quicker than writing, and hearing your ideas may get you in the mood to write.

2. Start writing the part of the document that comes most easily, or, depending on your makeup, start with the section that is most difficult. In either case, don't feel that you must write the segments in the order in which they will appear.

3. Have your draft typed if you write in longhand. Working

from typed copy will enable you to edit more quickly and to look more objectively at what you've written.

4. Avoid writing, if possible, when you are emotionally or mentally preoccupied.

5. Find the time of day and the place where you write most comfortably; surroundings can have a surprising influence on your readiness to write.

6. Promise yourself a reward for your hard work.

(Also see "Finding an Efficient Writing System" on page 12.)

3

Making Your Message Accessible

The Subject Line

Your aim in business writing should be to communicate as much information as clearly and concisely as you can. It is no virtue to have your readers read to the middle or end of a memo and only there discover what it is about. You can prevent such a communication breakdown by supplying an informative, specific, and interesting subject line.

The subject line on a business document serves the same purpose as a headline on a newspaper story: It engages the reader's interest. In writing the subject line, pull key words—specific action words—from the piece up to your headline. Make sure that the subject line is unambiguous and that it accurately represents what follows.

In routine memos, a topical heading such as "Agenda for October Meeting" or "Follow-up on Mailing List Survey" will suffice. In nonroutine memos, however, the subject line can do more than simply identify a broad area. It can also give specific information about the subject, limit and focus the memo, and even motivate the reader to read on. Notice how the second subject line in each pair below improves upon the first:

Re: Changing Discount Policies
Re: Increasing User Discounts by 15%

Re: Expense Accounts
Re: Procedures for Submitting Expense Vouchers

Re: New Equipment
Re: New Equipment Arouses Safety Concerns

When your reader can react to your subject line by asking, "What about it?" you haven't done your job. Be sure you answer the reader's question: "What about the new equipment?" "It has aroused safety concerns."

One exception is worth noting. If you anticipate that your reader will react negatively to a subject line, and if this is not your intent, write a more general one. "Revised Vacation Policy" is less alarming than "Cut in Vacation Days."

Beginnings

The only requirements for beginnings are that they be clear, purposeful, and direct. Your reader wants to know at once *why* you are writing and *what* you are writing about. Thus, you should begin by stating these essential points of information:

- The purpose.
- The subject.

Depending on your purpose and your reader's familiarity with a subject, you may want to include the following additional information:

- The context or background.
- The importance of the subject.

- An overview of the main points.
- The way the document is structured.
- Your conclusions and recommendations.

Not all these points need to be included, nor do they need to follow any particular order. In reading the three examples that follow, notice which points have been included and how they have been ordered:

Our recent merger requires that we adopt the personnel policies of our parent company. These policies are very different from the ones we have been operating under. Please review the comparisons set out in this report so that you will understand how the new policies affect you. Please call me if you need further explanation.

•

Thank you for inquiring about our savings plans. Either plan would be suitable for your account. I have explained below the costs for each plan and the differences between them.

•

Seventy percent of contractors who have substantially renovated office buildings in our county during the past five years have chosen electric heat over other heating sources. I recommend that you use electric heat when you renovate the Packard Building. This memo (1) describes all feasible sources of heat for the building, (2) explains why electric heat is best for your purposes, and (3) compares the cost of electric heat with other sources.

Conclusions—First or Last?*

Whenever you write a document that includes conclusions and recommendations, you must decide where to place them—at the beginning or at the end. Traditionally, writers have held conclusions off to the end. Today, however, in response to the demands on their reader's time and attention, writers begin with their conclusions, then justify them.

Knowing your reader's attitude toward your subject and toward you will help you decide where to put your conclusions. As a rule, the answers to the following questions will lead you to the right decision:

How interested is the reader in the subject?

If the reader has little or only moderate interest in the subject, announce your conclusions and recommendations immediately—lest the reader never get to them. If the reader is highly interested, you may delay them since he or she is likely to be as interested in the discussion as in the conclusions.

Does the reader have a bias toward your conclusions and recommendations?

If the reader is positively biased or neutral, lead with your conclusions and recommendations. If the reader is negatively biased, disclose them only after you have worn down his or her resistance by clearly and cogently arguing your position.

---

*Thanks to JoAnne Yates at the Sloan School of Management, Massachusetts Institute of Technology, for her ideas on this subject.

What is your credibility with the reader?

If you have high credibility, state your conclusions promptly. If your credibility is low, consider withholding them until you've built your strongest possible case.

If you are unable to gauge the predispositions of your reader, the odds today favor putting your conclusions at the beginning. The accelerated tempo of the times argues for letting readers know the results of your thinking immediately.

Endings

When you come to the end of a document, both you and your reader need a sense of closure. You must settle the business at hand and leave your reader with a strong final impression.

A good conclusion focuses on points that you want your reader to take away from your piece. Depending on the purpose and length of your document, you may do one or more of the following:

- Reiterate important points.
- State desired outcomes.
- Recommend actions to be taken.
- Suggest next steps.

The three examples below round out and pull together earlier parts of the document:

After December 15, you will have to wait an entire year to switch from one plan to another. Thus, if you wish to make a change, you must submit a completed application form before

December 15. Please call the Compensation Office (Extension 4378) to obtain a form.

●

Thus, leasing 10,000 square feet will provide you with the additional space you need. The first floor of the building at 1100 Wisconsin Avenue will be available for rental beginning September 1. It meets all your requirements and is in the price range you stipulated.

If you would like to see the space, I can arrange for you to see it. If you would like me to look for other rental space, I will be happy to do so. I will be in town all week and look forward to hearing from you.

●

I believe we should seek another vendor for these services immediately, for we cannot afford to have our image suffer from the low-quality work done by XCel Company. I am in the process of contacting other vendors and will provide you with a table comparing their services and prices.

Will you be free next Monday so that we can reach a decision on the matter?

Headings

Well-written headings serve important purposes. They enable readers to skim a piece of writing, get an overview of its contents, and focus on issues of interest. They enable you to highlight important points and break up long blocks of solid print.

Headings are not easy to write, for they must fulfill several requirements. Four major requirements are explained below.

Headings should show the relationship of ideas. By simply looking at a piece of writing, a reader should be able to tell which topics are of major, secondary, or minor importance. All topics at the same level of generalization should have headings that look the same; that is, their typography and placement should be identical. The typographic options available on most computer printers provide writers with a wide range of design choices. Headings can be underlined, printed in boldface, italics, all capitals, or set in a different typeface. Higher-level headings should have more visual impact than lower-level headings.

Headings should be informative. Just as the headings in newspapers provide readers with information, so too should the headings in business documents. A heading should give as much information as possible. The heading "Bright Future for Product X," for example, can be made more specific: "Sales of Product X to Double by 1995." Broad headings like "Background" and "Conclusion" should be replaced with headings that summarize the background ("Regulation Has Limited Our Marketing Efforts") or state the conclusion ("Deregulation Will Open New Markets").

Headings should match the information in scope. Headings should fit the material that follows them; they should be neither too broad nor too narrow. If a heading reads "Homeowners Protest Ruling," the discussion that follows should be limited to only that point. If those who rent property are also discussed, the heading should be broadened: "Residents Protest Ruling." If only owners of vacation homes protest the ruling, the heading should be narrowed: "Owners of Vacation Homes Protest Ruling."

Headings should be parallel. Headings at the same level should be grammatically parallel. For example, if a section of a report discusses problems that lie ahead, the headings must be in the same grammatical form: "Patent Expiring," "Market Share Decreasing," "Labor Force Shrinking." (See "Parallelism" on page 129.)

Notice how headings have been used in the sample letters and memos throughout this book.

Graphic Devices

Readers choose to read documents primarily because of the importance of the subject to them. Beyond that, they choose short pieces over long ones and those that look easy to read over those that look tedious.

The following devices will help you design a document that will attract and hold your reader's attention:

- White Space.
- Boldface.
- Bullets.
- Underlining.
- Capitals.

White space. The white space that surrounds the list above makes it stand out. (You probably skimmed the list before you began reading the introductory paragraph.) Using plenty of white space (generous margins and breaks between paragraphs) will make your document inviting.

Boldface. Double striking by a typewriter or computer printer makes a word or passage more noticeable. (Notice how the first word in this paragraph, and in the next three paragraphs, stands out.) Sometimes boldface does not reproduce well. If you are making multiple copies of a document, you may prefer to use a different device.

Bullets. Bullets (the black dots that precede the listed items on the previous page) are used to set off major points that can be expressed briefly. They are widely used in business because they telegraph important information quickly. (See "Bullets" on page 30 for guidelines on using bullets.)

Underlining. Underlining can also call the reader's attention to points that might otherwise be skimmed over.

Capitals. Single words or short passages may be printed in capital letters for emphasis. Warnings, changes in policy or procedures, a company name, or the name of a product are often printed in "all caps."

The layout of your document conveys a strong visual message to your reader. Use graphic devices to reinforce your verbal message. HIGHLIGHT ONLY IMPORTANT INFORMATION; otherwise the purpose for using graphic devices will be defeated—your reader will be distracted rather than engaged.

The bland format of the following report works against the reader's desire to read and remember it. Compare it to the revision, which has a better layout and a better beginning and end.

May 30, 1989

Today I met with Philip Delafon, CFO of Tyson Corporation. The meeting was intended to be of an introductory/exploratory nature since Philip and I had never met. We discussed many issues in our short meeting.

Philip needs a cash management service so that he can keep track of daily balances, including those at other banks. He's looked at First Federal and County Bank's services but was eager to hear about our Multibalance service. I tentatively scheduled a meeting for June 5 to explain the service in detail. I told him I'd try to get Emad Hassar to attend this meeting.

Philip mentioned three projects he'd like to fund through IRBs: a $1.5 million project to expand port facilities in Gloucester, a $1 million project to establish a warehouse in Essex, and a $7 million project to build a plant in Salisbury. Although First Federal has provided IRBs in the past, Philip said neither First Federal nor County Bank was interested in these deals. He understood our limited ability to absorb tax-free allocations. I turned down the $7 million plant but told him we'd fund the $2.5 million, subject to agreeable pricing.

Philip also mentioned that Tyson's union wants a guarantee for the company's annual $1 million payment to the pension fund. I explained how a standby letter of credit might guarantee this payment. I offered him a price of .050 - .075% for this L/C. He wants more information and a firm price.

BG
_____
Barbara Greyson
Assistant Vice-President

CALL REPORT

May 30, 1989
Tyson Corporation
<u>Met with Philip Delafon, CFO</u>

Today I met with Philip to introduce myself as the new officer on the account and to get a sense of Tyson's current banking needs. Discussion centered around cash management, IRBs, and a standby letter of credit.

Cash Management

Philip needs a cash management service so that he can keep track of daily balances, including those at other banks. He's looked at First Federal and County Bank's services but was eager to hear more about our Multibalance service. I tentatively scheduled a meeting for June 5 to explain the service in detail. I told him I'd try to get Emad Hassar to attend this meeting.

IRBs

Philip mentioned three projects he'd like to fund through IRBs:
- $1.5 million to expand port facilities in Gloucester.
- $1.0 million to establish a warehouse in Essex.
- $7.0 million to build a plant in Salisbury.

Although First Federal has provided IRBs in the past, Philip said neither First Federal nor County Bank was interested in these deals. He understood our limited ability to absorb tax-free allocations. I turned down the $7 million plant but told him we'd fund the $2.5 million, subject to agreeable pricing.

Standby Letter of Credit

Tyson's union wants a guarantee for the company's $1 million annual payment to the pension fund. I explained how a standby letter of credit might guarantee this payment. I offered him a price of .050 - .075% for this L/C. He wants more information and a firm price.

Follow-Up Steps

- Call Emad for 6/5 meeting.
- Propose a price and terms on IRBs.
- Check price on L/C with Ned. Write proposal for this business.

BG

_____

Barbara Greyson
Assistant Vice-President

Bullets

Bullets (black dots that precede listed items) are popular graphic devices. They help you emphasize key ideas and they help your reader extract those ideas quickly.

Bullets should be used sparingly, for if you overuse them, they will lose their impact and confuse the reader. He or she may fail to notice important ideas because other less important information is also highlighted by bullets.

Requirements of Bulleted Lists

Two requirements, based on the logic of outlining, apply to bullets: Bulleted points must be conceptually parallel, and they must be grammatically parallel.

Conceptual parallelism requires that the bulleted items be discrete, nonoverlapping ideas at the same level of specificity. In the following example, the fourth point is not conceptually parallel.

The task force identified several reasons for excessive breakage in shipping. Packers failed to do the following:
- Use heavy cartons.
- Pad the tubes adequately.
- Seal the cartons securely.
- Meet standards because of inadequate training.

The fourth point is more general than the other points and might, in fact, be the cause for the first three failings. It should be eliminated from the list. It could be included in the lead-in ("Because of inadequate training, packers failed to . . ."), or it could appear as a separate sentence following the list ("These packing standards were not met because packers have not been adequately trained").

Grammatical parallelism requires that each point be written in the same grammatical structure. The following list is conceptually parallel, but not grammatically parallel:

Each department head will be responsible for the following:
- Reducing overtime costs.
- An update of job descriptions.
- Provide training to new employees.

If all points began with an *-ing* word *(reducing, updating, providing),* the list would be grammatically parallel. (See "Parallelism," page 129.)

Guidelines for Bulleted Points

Because bullets are relatively new to business writing, no strict rules govern their usage. Some firms have style guides to ensure that everyone in the firm uses bullets the same way. If your firm has no such guidelines, follow these:

- Limit a sequence of bulleted points to just a few.
- Use bullets before phrases, sentences, or passages of only a few lines.
- Word each point succinctly.

Punctuation of bulleted points follows no set rules. In the examples above, and throughout this book, the style common to several major newspapers is used. Each point begins with a capital letter and ends with a period. Phrases and sentences are treated similarly. A colon follows the lead-in sentence.

An Easy-To-Read Style

Style in writing comprises many elements—organization, paragraph and sentence length and structure, and word choice. Style refers to the way your writing reads and sounds—the way you present your ideas.

An easy-to-read style allows readers to understand what you have written in one careful, but quick, reading. The piece should move along at a brisk, but natural, pace.

Though short words, short sentences, and short paragraphs will keep your reader from getting bogged down, they alone will not guarantee that your style is easy to read. Ideas must be well connected, and the rhythm must resemble the rhythm used in speech. Reading a piece of writing aloud may help you hear how it sounds. If it is hard to read aloud, it will be hard to read silently.

Compare the following passages. The ones to the left are harder to understand than the ones to the right.

The currency rates that are presently being used to calculate the revaluations made every month are not being compared to a designated independent source to determine whether they are accurate. Due to the fluctuating nature of currency rates, it is absolutely imperative that the rates used in the calculation be subject to a comparison to assure their accuracy.

Currency rates used to calculate the monthly revaluation are not being checked for accuracy against a reliable outside source. Because the rates fluctuate widely, such a comparison should be made.

In the next decade Citizens Airways is planning to purchase and begin operating several fully modern aircraft (five Boeing 747s, two DC-10-30s with stretched upper decks, and three 200-seat airbuses—all to be delivered in 1995), which will allow the company to increase domestic service by 15% and to begin penetrating the burgeoning international market. Its international service will increase by 40% as the new aircraft will be utilized on the traffic-intensive corridors of London, Paris, and Frankfurt. The increase in domestic service will be possible because of the new 747s.

Citizens Airways is planning to expand its service over the next decade. It has ordered five Boeing 747s, two DC-10-30s, and three 200-seat airbuses for delivery in 1995. The 747s will be used to expand domestic service; the DC-10s and the airbuses will be used to service the international routes that Citizens has just been awarded. These routes include London, Paris, and Frankfurt. When the new aircraft are operating, Citizens' domestic service will increase 15%. Its international service will increase 40%.

(Also see Chapter 5, pages 68–71 for more suggestions on style.)

Strengthening a Weak Memo

Read and compare the memos on pages 35 and 36. The first memo is weak and uninteresting. The layout does not invite reading. The purpose of the memo is not immediately clear. The writer takes his readers through his reasoning process, giving too much background and not enough details about the new program. The style is wordy and trite. The writer doesn't sound committed to the project, nor does he seem to know what he wants.

The second memo invites reading. It is quick, clear, and direct. The writer makes specific suggestions. He seems knowledgeable and interested in the project.

Country Clothes, ltd.   **INTEROFFICE MEMORANDUM**

To: Regional Sales Managers   March 29, 1989

From: Warren P. Chase, Vice President of Marketing WPC

Re: Change in Policy and Procedures

You are no doubt aware that we have made several changes in procedures over the past year. These changes have dealt with efforts to improve the efficiency of our internal operations.

Now that certain improvements have been instituted, we must turn our attention to other matters. In particular, we must look at the markets we are serving.

For many years we outfitted young adults aged 20 to 30 years old. These 20- and 30-year-olds have grown up, and, even though they are older, they want to continue dressing casually. Thus we must begin placing an emphasis on serving those in the 35 to 55 age group.

Please be advised that we will discuss this shift in emphasis at the quarterly meeting. Before then, begin thinking of ways you can begin this shift. Buyers will have to order different styles and sizes. Advertising and displays will have to be changed. Some personnel considerations also bear discussion.

Feel free to begin making any changes that will benefit your store and bring all your ideas to the meeting next month.

Country Clothes Ltd.

To: Regional Managers   March 29, 1989

From: Warren P. Chase, Vice President of Marketing W PC

Re: Shift in Marketing Emphasis

In the past we have targeted our marketing efforts to young adults, those 20 to 30 years old. Over the next year we will be shifting our emphasis to an older adult market—to those between 35 and 55.

RATIONALE. Until recently, young adults tended to dress more casually than those 35 and over; thus we catered to this market. Now, people of all ages dress casually; hence we need to serve a broader population. Moreover, the age mix of the population is changing. People aged 35 to 55 make up 25 percent of the population. This percentage will grow over the next decade and beyond.

IMPLEMENTATION. At our quarterly meeting we will discuss ways to implement a formal program; however, as you see opportunities to begin this shift, please take advantage of them. Consider making the following changes, as appropriate, in your region:

Buying. Advise your buyers of our revised strategy so that they can begin filling our racks and shelves with products that will appeal to this age group.

Sales Force. In hiring new sales personnel, hire mature adults as well as young adults. (Review Bulletin #6 on "Discrimination and Hiring Policies.") We want a balanced sales force.

Displays. In displaying products, both inside the stores and in windows, choose styles, colors, and fabrics that will appeal to this group.

Advertising. Ask your advertising agencies or departments to focus their efforts on reaching this age group. Have them place ads in media that are popular with this group.

This changeover should be gradual. We do not want to lose younger adults, but we want older adults to feel that our stores serve their needs as well.

At our meeting next month, please be prepared to talk about what you plan to do in your store. In the meantime, call me if you have any questions.

4

Shaping Paragraphs
and Sentences

Paragraph Focus and Topic Sentences

A paragraph is a group of sentences that develops only one idea or one part of an extended idea. This idea, or topic, is usually encapsulated in a sentence called "the topic sentence." The topic sentence defines just what can be covered in a paragraph. Staying within the boundaries of that topic sentence will ensure that your paragraph remains focused.

The topic sentence may appear anywhere in the paragraph or not at all. By putting it near the beginning, you let your readers know immediately what the paragraph is about. In business writing, the topic sentence should most often be placed at the beginning of the paragraph. By putting it near the end, you build up to your main idea. By not putting in a topic sentence, you assume that the central idea of your paragraph is so clear that it need not be stated.

The following paragraph focuses on a single idea. The topic sentence, the first sentence, limits the items that can be discussed to a very few:

Your securities are safe with your broker. All securities held for you by your brokerage firm are insured by Securities Investor

Protection Corporation, a congressionally chartered company. Your brokerage firm may also take out additional insurance from a commercial insurance company. If your brokerage firm goes under, you will not lose the securities it holds for you.

Notice how the addition of a few more ideas destroys the focus and flow of the paragraph and weakens its impact:

Your securities are safe with your broker. The securities your broker holds are not in your name but in "street name." The brokerage firm assigns these shares to your account. All securities held for you by your brokerage firm are insured by Securities Investor Protection Corporation, a congressionally chartered company. Your broker may also take out additional insurance from a commercial insurance company. If'your brokerage firm goes under, you will not lose the securities it holds for you. If your securities are in your own safe-deposit box, they are not automatically insured against fire or theft. You must take out your own insurance.

The second and third sentences in the paragraph above add irrelevant details and distract the reader from the point of the paragraph. The last two sentences dealing with keeping securities in a safe-deposit box also diverge from the central idea—safety in keeping securities with a broker. These last two sentences could remain in this paragraph if the topic sentence were broadened. It might read as follows: "Keeping securities with your broker might be safer than keeping them in a safe-deposit box."

The following paragraph focuses on a single idea. Notice how specific facts lead to the concluding statement, the topic sentence.

Next year Avondale will spend $150,000 more to dispose of its trash than it did two years ago. Last March skyrocketing disposal costs forced Glenbrook to raise the cost of a permit for bringing trash to a local transfer station from $1 to $125. Overall, the average cost of burning or burying garbage has tripled since 1980. As landfills close and incinerators fill to capacity, cities and towns are scrambling for places to dump their refuse. Residents of most communities are paying ever-higher prices to dispose of garbage in ever-fewer places.

The next paragraph contains no topic sentence as such, yet— except for one sentence that should be omitted—the paragraph holds together nicely:

The mall will be constructed on the site now occupied by the Plains Upholstery plant. It will consist of 250,000 square feet of retail space on two levels, 10,000 square feet of parking space, and 10,000 square feet of outdoor recreation space. Swartz Management is now trying to attract tenants to the mall. Construction will begin in August; the mall will be ready for occupancy next June.

The second-to-last sentence ("Swartz Management is . . .") diverges from the main focus of the paragraph—construction plans for the new mall.

When you are drafting a piece of writing, ideas may come to you so quickly that you do not want to take the time to sort them into neat, well-focused paragraphs. But when you come back to revise, make sure that each paragraph holds together as a unit and that your topic sentence helps define what the paragraph is about.

Paragraph Development

Some writers fail to appreciate the importance of substantiating their ideas with supporting facts or explanations. Their readers get interested in the subject only to be disappointed when no further information is provided. Other writers get so carried away with a subject that they go into too much detail. Their readers get bored or stop reading. Thus, when you write, you will have to decide how thoroughly to develop your ideas.

If an idea is important to your discussion, take the time to develop it adequately, but not excessively. The kind and amount of development will vary according to your purpose and your reader's level of knowledge and interest.

The following paragraph appeared in a brochure put out by a bank. Its purpose was to interest customers in taking out a home-improvement loan. The paragraph needs to be further developed:

> Home improvements enhance the appearance of a home, make it more comfortable, and add to its resale value. In general, the longer you live in your house, the more your home improvements will be worth in the future.

Adding specific examples to the paragraph above makes it more interesting and more convincing:

> Home improvements enhance the appearance of a home, make it more comfortable, and add to its resale value. In general, the longer you live in your house, the more your home improvements will be worth in the future. By modernizing a kitchen or bathroom, you can expect a return of from 80 to 125 percent on your initial investment upon resale. By making your house more energy-efficient, you can recoup from 60 to 75 percent on your investment, in addition to the money you will save on heating and cooling costs. By improving the exterior of your home—doors, windows, roofing, landscaping—you can get back from 50 to 75 percent of your investment.

If the paragraph were to go into much more detail, it might not hold the interest of the general reader.

(See "Paragraph Focus and Topic Sentences" on pages 37–39 for other examples of paragraphs that are adequately developed.)

Paragraph Length

Readers today are more used to reading short paragraphs than long ones. Indeed, many readers are put off by long paragraphs, for they make a piece of writing look tedious and boring.

If a paragraph runs more than ten to twelve lines (about two inches long), you should consider breaking it into two or more paragraphs, even if it develops a single idea.

The length of a paragraph depends on the information it conveys. If you were writing a one-page memo relaying several unrelated facts, you would probably write several short paragraphs, one for each fact. If you were writing a report in which you were explaining detailed concepts, your paragraphs would be longer because the flow of the discussion would hold your reader's interest. If you were writing a transitional paragraph, it might be only two or three sentences long. Occasionally, if you wanted an idea to stand out, you could write a single-sentence paragraph.

When a paragraph gets too long, look for logical points at which to begin a new paragraph. Sometimes the breaking points are obvious; sometimes they are arbitrary. The following paragraph, for example, can be broken at various places:

The request for a $400,000 increase in the budget for Phase I is justified. Construction costs have increased about $10,000 per unit because the majority of buyers are upgrading the basic unit by purchasing options that were not calculated in the initial construction budget. The options include brickfacing the fireplaces, installing storm and screen doors, and painting the interior of the garages. These add-ons account for $300,000 in additional funding. The remaining $100,000 would be spent on related costs. Approximately $50,000 would be spent to pay for additional labor and overtime costs; $40,000 would be spent to upgrade the model units; $10,000 would be spent to reissue brochures and literature describing the model unit. We should make these funds available by the end of the month.

A new paragraph could begin with the fourth sentence ("These add-ons . . .") or with the fifth sentence ("The remaining $100,000 . . ."). If the writer wanted to make the last sentence emphatic, it could stand as a separate paragraph.

In deciding where to break a paragraph, first find logical points at which to break. Then see how well each new paragraph holds together. Look at the information that precedes and follows the paragraph in question, and look at the length of surrounding paragraphs. (Variety in length is desirable.) Parcel out the information into manageable units, each of which retains a focus while connecting well to the paragraphs that precede and follow.

Sentence Length and Rhythm

Vary the structure and length of your sentences so that the rhythm and pace of your writing does not become monotonous. In the following passage the ideas unfold too slowly. Sentences are similar not only in length but also in structure:

The current turnover among operators who work at Video Display Terminals (VDTs) is 55%. The turnover rate for other clerical personnel is 40%. The cost to hire and train one new VDT operator is $1,200. We now spend $180,000 annually on training new operators. We can reduce this cost by a substantial amount. I am proposing a pilot program that can help us deal with the problem. This memo describes that program.

The following passage demonstrates a different problem:

Since our turnover rate for Video Display Terminal (VDT) operators is 55% compared to 40% for other clerical personnel, and, since each new operator hired costs us $1,200 a year, training these operators requires our division to spend $180,000 a year, a figure that can be reduced by implementing the pilot program I propose in this memo.

This version is overly compressed. The reader must collect and retain a lot of information—and will inevitably have to reread the passage.

The ideal, of course, is to allow ideas to flow at just the right rate. Readers literally need to blink to lubricate their eyes. Mixing the length and structure of sentences results in a pleasing, easy-to-read rhythm:

The turnover rate for operators of Video Display Terminals (VDTs) is 55% compared to 40% for other clerical workers. Hiring and training a new operator costs us $1,200 per employee, or $180,000 annually. To reduce this expense, I propose we implement the following pilot program.

Reading your writing aloud (or having someone read it aloud to you) will give you a sense of the rhythm. If your sentences fall into too steady a singsong pattern, you will want to revise them. Similarly, if you find yourself gasping for breath, while the period sits at some distance ahead, you will want to revise the passage. By varying the structure and length of your sentences, you can keep your readers from being lulled to sleep or from being tired out.

Sentences Joined by *And*

And is frequently used to join two sentences. It is used correctly when it joins two related ideas of equal importance:

The president is in Tokyo, and the treasurer is in Paris.
Volume has increased, and prices have dropped.

And is used incorrectly, however, when it joins two ideas that bear a more complex relationship than that signified by *and*. (*And* simply signals an additional thought.) If one idea is causal or conditional, or if a time sequence is suggested, *and* should not be used. Note the following revisions:

CAUSAL   Profits increased 15% last quarter, and we'll get a bonus.
Because profits increased 15% last quarter, we'll get a bonus.

Routing slips were lost, and our shipments will be delayed.
The loss of the routing slips will delay our shipments.

CONDITIONAL   Lower your overhead, and your profits will increase.
If you lower your overhead, profits will increase.

Send me the spreadsheet, and I'll check the figures.
If you send me the spreadsheet, I'll check the figures.

TIME
SEQUENCE   All bills have been paid, and we know we stayed within budget.
Now that all bills have been paid, we know that we stayed within budget.

He arrived in Atlanta and realized he had lost the report.
When he arrived in Atlanta, he realized he had lost the report.

In rereading your draft, circle every *and*. Question its use. Does *and* obscure a more complex relationship between ideas?

Hard-To-Read Sentences

Business readers should be able to read a sentence once and understand it. Short sentences are generally easier to follow than long ones, but even long sentences can be easy to read if they are structured carefully. To keep long sentences from becoming unwieldy, (1) retain normal word order (subject-verb-object), (2) keep the subject and verb close to one another, or (3) set off the intervening material clearly.

1. Retain normal word order.

In this sentence three objects come first, followed by the verb, and finally the subject:

> Careless circling of the unit of measure, incorrect or missing code numbers, and misspelled customer names were the most common mistakes.

The sentence communicates more quickly if the subject-verb-object pattern is retained:

> The most common errors were (a) careless circling of the unit of measure, (b) incorrect or missing code numbers, and (c) misspelled customer names.

The following sentence should also be revised to retain normal word order:

> A raise he has asked for and a raise he will get.
> He has asked for a raise and he will get one.

2. Keep the subject and verb close to one another.

The subject comes at the very beginning of the next sentence. The verb comes at the very end:

Production increases resulting from the growing use of digital technology, electronic switching, and fiber optics, coupled with a projected 5.6% gain in telephones in service, will aid profits.

In the revision, the sentence is broken into two sentences. The verbs are closer to their subjects:

An increase in production and a projected 5.6% gain in telephones in service will aid profits. The increase in production will result from the growing use of digital technology, electronic switching, and fiber optics.

In the next sentence, 19 words come between the subject and verb:

Big Tin Company, despite its diversification into aluminum recycling and resource recovery, businesses that have done well over the last two years, has continued to lose market share to competition.

One way to revise the sentence is to put the verb immediately after the subject:

Big Tin Company has continued to lose market share to competition, despite its diversification into aluminum recycling and resource recovery—businesses that have done well over the last two years.

3. Set off the intervening material clearly.

The sentence above about the Big Tin Company can also be revised by setting the interrupting material off with dashes:

Big Tin Company—despite its diversification into aluminum recycling and resource recovery, businesses that have done well over the last two years—has continued to lose market share to competition.

If you tend to write sentences like the hard-to-read ones above, take pity on your readers. Revise the sentences into manageable, easy-to-read units.

Connecting Sentences and Paragraphs

Your writing will be quick and easy to read if sentences and paragraphs flow gracefully. The order of ideas within sentences and paragraphs obviously affects the flow. A number of explicit transitional devices can also provide the connections that will make your writing coherent.

Connecting Sentences

When you speak, you connect ideas quite naturally by repeating *key words* or by using *synonyms* and *pronouns*. The same transitional devices can help you connect sentences when you write.

Notice how these devices (underlined in the paragraph below) help join ideas:

Last month we surveyed customers in the Long Branch store to see if they liked the electronic scanning system at our checkout counters. The results of this survey showed that 83% of our customers liked the system (1) because they felt confident that they were charged the correct amount and (2) because they felt that the system allowed for quicker checkouts. On the basis of this study, we will expand the use of scanners to our other stores in the state.

You may also use some of the following *transitional words and expressions* to link your thoughts. The choice of the correct transition depends, of course, on the relationship of the two ideas:

ADDITION	and, in addition, also, too, furthermore, moreover
SEQUENCE	first, second, then, next, finally, now, later, before, after
COMPARISON	similarly, likewise, in comparison
CONTRAST	but, however, though, nevertheless, yet, on the other hand
ILLUSTRATION	for example, in particular, for instance, that is, specifically
RESULT	therefore, because, accordingly, consequently, thus, hence, as a result
SUMMARY	to sum up, in summary, in conclusion, finally
EMPHASIS	most important, chiefly, indeed, surely, of course
CORRELATION	either . . . or, neither . . . nor, not only . . . but also

A final device, repeating the same sentence structure in several sentences (parallelism), can help your ideas flow rhythmically. (See "Parallelism" on page 129.)

The transitional expressions and parallelism in the following paragraph make it easy to read and follow:

We will not meet our target date for implementing the new system <u>because</u> departments have failed to cooperate <u>and because</u> two vendors have failed to ship equipment on time. We can, <u>however,</u> be operational by March 15 if we take the <u>following</u> steps immediately: <u>First, we should encourage department heads to discuss</u> the situation <u>and to appoint</u> a liaison to improve interdepartmental interaction. <u>Second, we should contact the vendors</u> who are supplying equipment <u>to make sure</u> their delivery dates are firm. Third, we should budget funds to train all personnel in the new operation so that no further delays will occur when we convert to the new system. As a result of taking these steps we can surely be up and running before our busy season.

Connecting Paragraphs

The kinds of transitional devices that work well between sentences also work well between paragraphs. They quickly, and unobtrusively, link paragraphs. In some cases, however, you may need a more explicit transition. If you have explained the advantages of a plan in one paragraph, the next paragraph might begin this way: "Although the plan has several advantages, it also has some disadvantages."

In writing a transitional sentence, simply summarize what has gone before and anticipate what is to come. Avoid using such transitional sentences to link paragraphs that follow one another quite naturally. Too many transitions can be as annoying as too few.

When you take great leaps in thought, you might even need to write a short transitional paragraph. In the following example, the writer has spent several paragraphs discussing a time-saving method to collect samples. He now shifts to a discussion of the longer-than-normal testing phase.

> Although the new equipment will allow us to collect samples in half the time it now takes, testing these samples will still be a time-consuming task. In fact, because new procedures for testing will become necessary, testing may take up to 20 percent longer to perform.

Besides verbal signals, you can also use visual signals—headings and subheadings. A heading will let your reader know that you have come to the next stage of your discussion. The heading alone may suffice, or you may want to add a short transitional sentence as well. (Look back at the two subheadings used in this chapter and at the sentences that follow the subheadings.)

Transitional words, sentences, and paragraphs help your readers know where you are going. If your direction is obvious, you do not need to use a transitional device, but if your readers stand a chance of getting lost or delayed, signal the turns you are taking in your thought.

5

Editing for Language, Style, and Tone

Editing Is a Must

According to H. L. Mencken, an authority on language and a prolific writer himself, only 0.8 percent of the human race is capable of writing something that is instantly understandable. Unless you're part of that minuscule minority, editing is a must.

Editing means reviewing what you have written for its effect on the reader, not simply changing a word here, a comma there. Although editing does take time and effort, it will help you produce writing that will show you at your best.

When you edit your work, put yourself in the reader's place. Ask the questions your reader might ask: "What does this word mean? Why didn't you tell me that fact sooner? Why are you boring me with all these details? What do you want? How much will it cost?" By adopting your reader's point of view, you may be more objective than you might otherwise be.

Whenever possible, try not to edit your draft soon after you've written it. Getting away from it for a time may help you see its strengths and weaknesses. (If you've ever come upon something you wrote a year or two ago, you can appreciate how important the passage of time is in changing your perceptions about a piece of writing.)

The following checklist can help you edit your writing methodically. The list is organized into five broad areas. Try to make five quick passes through your draft, focusing on one area at a time, rather than looking for everything in a single pass.

A Checklist for Editing

CONTENT

Keeping the intended reader in mind, is the information complete? Is it accurate?

Should any information be added, deleted, modified?

Are the points adequately, but not excessively, developed?

ORGANIZATION AND LAYOUT

Will the reader know immediately what you are writing about?

Would the information be more effective if it were reorganized?

Is there a logical order in the way the ideas are presented?

Is the layout appealing? Does it highlight important points?

PARAGRAPH STRUCTURE

Does each paragraph make one major point?

Is each major point explicitly stated?

Can long paragraphs be divided or short ones combined?

STYLE AND TONE

Is the language specific, natural, and appropriate to the reader?

Can unnecessary words and phrases be deleted?

Are sentences varied in structure and in length?

Is the piece direct, clear, easy to read?

Does it flow smoothly?

Will the tone help you achieve your purpose?

MECHANICS

Is the grammar correct throughout?

Is the punctuation correct throughout?

Are all words spelled correctly?

Avoiding Language That Is Outdated or Faddish

If you want your writing to sound crisp and contemporary, you will have to avoid using words and expressions that, while once considered standard, are now considered outdated. If you want to sound businesslike, you'll also have to avoid using faddish or trendy words that may fall out of use as quickly as they came into use. Thousands of words lie between these two extremes. Using them will help you achieve a style that is both up-to-date and professional.

Outdated words and phrases. Business words and expressions borrowed from an earlier generation can make your writing sound artificial or pedantic. Every letter will read like a form letter, and you will sound bored or, even worse, boring. Thinking up substitute phrases is easy if you put your mind to it. Consider some of these revisions:

We acknowledge receipt of	We have received *or* Thank you for
As per your request	As you requested
Attached herewith	I am attaching
Enclosed please find	I am enclosing
It has come to my attention	I have noticed *or* I have been told
Hereinafter	Later
Please be advised that	Both these expressions can be
Hereby	eliminated

Fad words. New words come into language when they provide a meaning that existing words do not express. Many new words are born of new technology, events, or life-styles ("byte," "lift-off," "triple bypass," "day care," "windsurfing"). Once coined, new words can help you express yourself more clearly, succinctly, and colorfully. But if you use words that have not yet become current (words that are not yet listed in the latest edition of a good dictionary), you can confuse readers. If readers are unable to construe the meaning of a word, they will supply their own meaning or they will ignore the idea entirely. In either case, clarity and precision suffer.

A sampling of memos distributed recently in various firms yielded these curiosities:

Production of the machines is *ramping up.*
Will you *bottom-line* that for me?
Please *line through* any information that does not apply.
I don't see any *windows* for the next two weeks.
If your firm *partners* with us, we will divide profits equally.
Calendar these important dates.

What are the dangers of using such words in correspondence? First, readers may not understand precisely what you mean. (What does "ramping up" mean? Does to "bottom-line" mean to calculate the costs or the profits?) Second, even if readers understand the meaning, such words may slow their reading. (It takes a second reading to figure out what "line through," "windows," "partners," and "calendar" mean.) Third, your style may be inconsistent. (See "Consistency in Your Choice of Words" on page 57.) Last, you may come across as sounding less than professional.

In reviewing your draft, look at the words you have chosen. When you come upon words—either very old or very new— that you would never use in polite business or social conversation, rid your writing of them, too.

Using Words That Are Familiar and Concrete

If you are serious about making your writing clear, you will have to question the words you use and eliminate any that your readers might misunderstand, or not understand. You should not talk down to your readers, but neither should you try to impress them with your command of the language. (Most readers are unimpressed with such displays.) If you get your message across as simply and specifically as you can, you may impress them with the efficiency and clarity of your style.

Use Familiar Words

If you use familiar words, your readers will be able to read at their normal pace. But if you use specialized terms or unusual words, your readers will have to slow down or puzzle over them.

Every field uses its own specialized language. Bankers speak of "T-Bonds"; computer experts speak of "booting up the computer"; environmental scientists speak of an "ecosystem."

When writing or editing, constantly remind yourself of who your readers are. If they will understand specialized vocabulary, use it. If they might not, define the words or choose other, more familiar words. Thus the banker might want to recommend "U.S. Treasury Bonds" to a customer. The computer expert would tell a neophyte to "turn on the computer," and the environmental scientist might explain the specialized term: "In an ecosystem, a community consisting of all the organisms living in a place, . . ."

Since it is easy to slip into jargon without realizing it, let someone outside your field read your draft. Ask that person to circle every word or phrase that is troublesome. Then make those ideas clear to your reader.

Besides avoiding specialized vocabulary, avoid using uncommon words. Some readers, however well educated, may have limited vocabularies. Other readers, even if they have extensive vocabularies, do not want to expend much mental energy reading business documents.

The length of a word is not necessarily at issue here. Many long words are familiar *(cooperation, circumstance, conversationalist),* while many short ones are not *(cant, carp, cull).* But if two words, one long and one short, have the same meaning and are equally familiar, choose the shorter word. Your style will be less high-sounding and easier to read.

Compare the following pairs of sentences:

Once he becomes acclimated to the department, he will be more amicable.

Once he becomes used to the department, he will be more friendly.

The hiring embargo will be a bane to the department.

The hiring freeze will be a burden to the department.

The second sentence in each pair above uses familiar words. The sentences read well. The first sentence in each pair tries too hard. The sentences are stilted.

Write to inform, not to show off or to test the vocabulary of your readers.

Use Concrete Words

Words can be concrete, that is, specific; or abstract, that is, general. The phrase "as soon as possible" is vague. "By tomorrow at 4:00 P.M." is specific. "Considerable savings" is vague. "A savings of $1,000 per month" is concrete.

In speaking of its Certificates of Deposit, a bank brochure states that they are written "for large amounts and relatively short maturities." How are readers to know what is meant by the abstract words *large* and *short?*

Abstract words, like abstract art, are open to the reader's interpretation. One person reading the bank brochure might consider putting $400,000 in a certificate as a week-long rest-ing place for some funds, while another may consider tucking away $500 for a trip to Europe in several years.

As ideas become more specific, they also become more interesting and informative. The second sentence in each pair below is far more concrete, and more interesting, than the first:

Security must be strengthened.
Passes must be checked at each entrance to the facility.

We will improve our large motors in the near future.
Within six months, our engineers will redesign engines over 500 horsepower so that they can operate continuously for up to ten days.

Sometimes you will want to make all-encompassing statements. You will want to use general words *(wealthy, assets, equipment)* instead of more concrete terms *(a millionaire, real-estate holdings, six double-sided disks)*. Whenever possible, be specific. You will save your reader from misinterpreting, or having to question, vague generalities.

Writers who are unsure of their message, or of their ability to write, often choose vague and unfamiliar words. By not pinning down ideas, these writers may feel that they are not really accountable for the message or for their writing. When you sit down to write, make sure you know what you want to say. Then say it as simply and precisely as you can.

Consistency in Your Choice of Words

Linguists commonly categorize language as formal, standard, or informal. Achieving a consistent style requires that you choose words at the same level of formality.

In formal prose, words like *inquisitive, loquacious, to censure* are common. In standard prose, the everyday synonyms—*curious, talkative, to criticize*—would be used. In very informal prose, the slang or colloquial equivalents—*nosy, gabby, to pick on*—might be used.

Formal English is rarely called for in the business world. It is usually reserved for academic or literary writing. Its vocabulary often sounds pretentious. It requires greater effort to read than standard English. Standard English is the language used by most educated writers most of the time. It tends to be more concrete than formal English and thus is suited to the action-oriented world of business. It communicates clearly without calling attention to itself. Informal English, including slang, is relaxed and casual. It may be appropriate if you know your reader well and if your subject is not weighty.

Revising for Consistency

In the following excerpt, notice the inconsistency in the level of words used:

> When senior management and the undersigned last met with Robert Troy, he asked that we consider granting his company a loan for $10 million so that it could begin expanding into the profitable southern markets. In making our decision we perused the company's financial statements for the past five years and also touched base with the company's accountant to ascertain the intended pay-back period. Since everything checked out, we called Mr. Troy and rendered our approval of the loan. Extension of the loan warrants quick action, especially since it's in the wind that he has also contacted other banks.

The passage should be revised for consistency:

When senior management and I met with Robert Troy, he asked that we consider granting his company a loan for $10 million so that it could begin expanding into the profitable southern markets. In making our decision we <u>studied</u> the company's financial statements for the past five years and also <u>spoke with</u> the company's accountant to <u>determine</u> the intended pay-back period. Since everything <u>was in good order</u>, we called Mr. Troy and <u>told him</u> we had approved the loan. Extension of the loan <u>demands</u> quick action since it has been <u>rumored</u> that he has also contacted other banks.

Before you write, decide on the appropriate level of language. As you edit, look for words that diverge from that level. Revise them so that your language will be consistent.

(Also see "Avoiding Language That Is Outdated or Faddish" on page 53.)

A Style for the Times

Perhaps no change in business writing in the last several decades has been so dramatic as the change in style. The principles of good writing have changed little. Writing must still be clear, cogent, and coherent. Paragraphs must still be unified and adequately developed. Sentences must still be constructed according to the rules of syntax, and grammar and punctuation must still be correct. But style, once indirect, has become direct; once protracted, has become brisk; once stiff, has become relaxed.

The style of our writing reflects the style of our work lives and of our personal lives. The efficiency brought by state-of-the-art technology has affected the way we do business and the way we communicate. The openness in the way we relate to others has affected the way we communicate with them. The changeover can be seen in the way a piece of writing looks, in the way it is structured, in its length, language, and tone.

Business writing no longer presents the reader with solid masses of print. Long blocks of prose are broken up into more manageable units. Headings and graphic devices (underlining, boldface, bulleted lists) make it easy to skim and easy to read.

Few letters begin at the beginning and take their readers to the end. Instead, they begin where they used to end—with conclusions and recommendations. The conclusions and recommendations are then explained or justified. Because of this change in structure, the approach, or style, has become direct, vigorous.

Some firms require that memos be one page or shorter. Some consultants, so the story goes, who used to supply a hefty report to justify their fees, now supply a slim summary report or no report at all. Executive summaries (short synopses of reports) now accompany reports, which are as short as they can possibly be. The length of paragraphs and sentences has also decreased.

Formal language has been replaced by the everyday language used in business. Tone, while still courteous, is less artificial, more sincere.

These changes respond to the needs of today's readers—decision makers down the hall who need to act quickly, or clients and customers who are finally proclaiming their right to understand information that affects them.

Achieving an Effective Style

Your writing style can be termed "effective" if it is (1) appropriate to the context and purpose of a document, and (2) appropriate to the audience.

Your style of writing can vary just as your mode of dress can vary. Sometimes you'll want to be proper and well dressed; at other times you'll want to be relaxed and casual. When writing a proposal to the executive committee, you'll want your style to be more formal than when you're writing a memo to a colleague asking for a simple favor. One style will simply be more "dressed up" than the other.

The range of acceptable styles in business writing is broad. Two extremes should be avoided—a stiff, overly formal style and a breezy, overly colloquial style. Your style should be professional but not stiff, warm but not cute. Your wardrobe, or repertoire of styles, should suit the occasions for which you write.

See the examples that follow. (Also see "An Easy-To-Read Style" on page 32.)

The style of the letter on the facing page is ineffective, for it is inappropriate to its purpose (to get a copy of an annual report) and to its reader (anyone who opens the letter). One sentence ("Please send me a copy of your latest annual report") would suffice.

3600 Connecticut Avenue NW
Washington, DC 20008
April 1, 1989

Dear Sir:

You are probably aware that there is quite some degree of variability in the informational content of annual reports of companies. Recognizing this variability, we are studying several characteristics of corporations that are associated with the extent of disclosure and propose to apply them to a carefully selected sample of companies. The companies in our sample have been chosen purely on the basis of their satisfying certain asset size and industrial representation requirements specified by us with a view to enabling meaningful comparisons to be made. Given this sample set of companies, the next stage of our analysis requires a careful study of their annual reports.

Your company is one of the companies in our sample. We would, therefore, appreciate it if you could send us a copy of your company's annual report for the latest financial year end. Your early response to this request should greatly facilitate the successful completion of this research project whose results, we believe, should be of aid in improving the content of annual reports.

Sincerely,

Winston Chapman. III

Winston Chapman, III

The style of the memo* on the opposite page is appropriate to its purpose (to explain the reversal of entrance and exit doors) and to its readers (users of the library). It is refreshing in its simplicity. It uses familiar words, personal pronouns, and a conversational approach.

*Used with permission of Edgar W. Davy, Dewey Library, Massachusetts Institute of Technology.

The Libraries
Massachusetts Institute of Technology
Cambridge, Massachusetts, 02139

Dewey Library
Room E53-100

19 April 1985

To: Puzzled Patrons of Dewey Library

Why on earth did we reverse the entrance and exit doors? Are we out of our minds, or something? Actually, the reversal is a by-product of the computer age, which was not foreseen by the architects of the building when it was built in 1965.

We will be installing computer terminals at the Dewey Circulation Desk before the end of next year. However, the 3M Security System cannot successfully coexist near the computer terminals, and vice versa.

Therefore, we had two choices. One solution would have been to rebuild the entire lobby wall to achieve the required distance between the security system and the computers. The other solution was to reverse the entrance and exit doors, which is what we did, as you may have noticed.

We hope you are getting used to the new system. We apologize for the inconvenience.

The Dewey Library Staff

The style of the letter on the adjacent page is appropriate to its purpose (to respond to a request for information on an environmental issue) and to its audience (the superintendent of the Water Department). It is simple, clear, and matter-of-fact. The style is more formal than that of the previous memo.

TISWELL ENGINEERING ^^^^^^

9 Shady Way
Westford, MA, 01886
(508) 692-4400

January 18, 1989

Stanley Whittier
Superintendent
Brittleton Water Department
Brittleton, MA 02567

Dear Superintendent:

At your request I have investigated the reasons for the heavy sodium content in the water coming from the Crystal Brook Reservoir. The reservoir is accumulating high amounts of sodium from two major sources:
   (1) salting and de-icing of the state highways within the watershed, and
   (2) an unprotected salt storage yard in Arbor, near the interchange of Routes 95 and 3.

The DPW will be meeting with the City of Brittleton officials on January 28. At this meeting they will discuss options available to reduce sodium levels. The DPW has tried using a chemical mixture for de-icing operations. It will share the results of their preliminary tests at that time. It is also considering installing a new roadway drainage system on Route 95 that will collect all water runoff and de-icing brine solution. The runoff would be diverted to Edwards River. The new system could be installed during the reconstruction of the Brittleton/Arbor section of Route 95 scheduled for next spring.

The DPW also intends to change the way it stores salt in the Arbor yard. The salt will now be kept in storage containers; thus leakage from the salt that is presently stored in the open should be eliminated.

Controlling these sources should bring the level of sodium in water from the Crystal Brook Reservoir down to healthy levels. I will be following up with the DPW after its meeting later this month and will let you know what is decided at that meeting.

If you would like the details of my study, I shall be happy to provide them.

Sincerely,

Dana Aubouchon

Dana Aubouchon
Engineering Consultant

Tightening Your Style

I have written you a long letter because I have not had time to write you a short one.

This quotation (attributed to Pascal, among others) encapsulates an ironic truth. But the time you spend tightening your writing will be time well spent. Writers who are brief are perceived to be more decisive and confident than those who are verbose.

If you compress your message, you will endear yourself to most readers. A short document is more likely to be read than a longer one, and it is often easier to understand and remember.

The most obvious way to be brief is to eliminate information. Omit unessential background or details. Make sure every bit of information contributes to your message. Do not feel compelled to tell everything you know about a subject. Focus on the points your reader needs.

Once you have eliminated unessential information, go through each sentence getting rid of unnecessary words. Professional editors usually look for certain kinds of words or grammatical structures that force writing to become wordy. If you want your style to be brief and vigorous, become aware of the places to look for wordiness:

WHO AND *WHICH* CLAUSES

The use of *who* and *which* may force you to use more words than necessary:

> Salaries *which* are paid to teachers comprise 65% of the school budget.
>
> Teachers' salaries comprise 65% of the school budget.

Daniel Stoddard, *who* is our dean of Academic Affairs, will call you.

Daniel Stoddard, dean of Academic Affairs, will call you.

PREPOSITIONAL PHRASES

Commonly used prepositions include *across, after, as, at, before, between, by, for, from, in, on, over, through, to, under, until, with.* Prepositions are important function words, for they connect one idea to another, but if they are overused, they can cause sentences to become stringy:

In the event *of* a price increase, we will renegotiate the contract we have *with* you.

If prices increase, we will renegotiate our contract.

The increase *in* investments *by* foreign nations is *of* concern *to* many economists.

Increased investment by foreign nations concerns many economists.

Be careful not to string together too many words just to avoid using a prepositional phrase, however. Clarity is more important than brevity.

The manager plans to support company budget-planning activities.

The manager plans to support the budget-planning activities of the company.

Many common expressions containing prepositions can be tightened:

in regard to = about	along the lines of = like
as soon as = when	due to the fact that = because
at a later date = later	at the present time = now
by means of = by	for the purpose of = for

REDUNDANCIES

Some banks offer "free gifts." Some insecticides "kill bugs dead." Develop an eye and an ear for detecting redundancies or repetitious expressions:

advance planning	final outcome	new innovation
past history	refer back	desirable benefits
necessary requisites	large in size	consensus of opinion
basic fundamentals	end results	future projections

THE VERB *TO BE*

Be, am, is, are, was, were, been, being are forms of the verb *to be.* Besides forcing wordiness, the verb *to be* is weak. (Notice below how prepositions sometimes attach themselves to the verb *to be.*)

The company *is* engaged in the processing of liquified gas.
The company processes liquified gas.

She *is* in a position to enforce the policy.
She can enforce the policy.

It *was* our advice that he find another job.
We advised him to find another job.

THERE IS AND *THERE ARE*

There is and *There are* should be eliminated from the beginnings of sentences if they steal the important opening position from other more important words:

There is a possibility that performance reviews may be delayed.
Performance reviews may be delayed.

There are many reasons why we should delay the announcement.

We should delay the announcement for many reasons.

NOUNS THAT COULD BE VERBS

Many nouns (typically those ending in *-tion, -sion, -ance, -ence,
-ment, -ing*) can be replaced by their verb forms. (Notice how
prepositions attach themselves to some nouns.)

The committee took into considera*tion* the adop*tion* of the
proposal.

The committee considered adopting the proposal.

When we held the meet*ing,* the vice-president made the deci-
sion that the committee should take ac*tion* immediately.

When we met, the vice-president decided that the committee
should act immediately.

WEAK VERBS THAT COULD BE REPLACED
BY STRONGER VERBS

Several weak verbs *(make, take, give, have, bring, hold)* derive
meaning only if they couple with a noun (especially those
nouns ending with the suffixes mentioned above). Instead of
using these weak verbs, change the accompanying noun to its
verb form, or think of a more precise verb:

make a decision = decide	*make* a recommendation = recommend
take action = act	*take* into consideration = consider
give a response to = respond	*give* a promotion to = promote
have a tendency to = tend	*have* an ability to = can
bring to an end = end	*bring* to a resolution = resolve
hold a meeting = meet	*hold* a conference = confer

Active and Passive Verbs

Passive verbs have lessened the impact of the following well-known sayings and quotations:*

> My heart was left by me in San Francisco.
> Only one life is had by me to be given to my country.
> "Cheese" should be said.
> Frankly, my dear, a damn isn't given by me.

Passive verbs can distort or have the same dulling effect on your writing. Whenever possible, use active verbs.

In an active sentence, the one who performs an action (the doer) precedes the verb:

> The clerk filed the applications.
> Gold Coast Properties earned money for the first time this quarter.

In a passive sentence, the doer appears at the end of the sentence, or not at all:

> The applications were filed by the clerk.
> The applications were filed.
> Money was earned for the first time this quarter by Gold Coast Properties.

Because the normal word order (subject-verb-object) is reversed in passive sentences, they are sometimes hard to follow. Because the doer of an action is sometimes omitted, the sentence may be vague or ambiguous. Passive sentences are longer and less vigorous than active sentences.

Passive verbs consist of the verb *to be* in any of its forms *(be,*

---

*Some clever person—who, I do not know—thought up these sentences. I found them among my vast collection of materials on writing. I hope the author will not mind my using them.

am, is, are, was, were, been, being) plus the past participle, or third form of the verb *(sing, sang, sung).* It's easy to make a passive sentence active. Simply begin the sentence with the subject, the "who" or "what" of the sentence. If you have omitted a doer, supply one when you revise the sentence:

Passive: Budgetary limits *were set* by Congress.
Active: Congress set budgetary limits.

Passive: The new contract *was fought.*
Active: The union fought the new contract.

Some writers use passive verbs because they are hesitant to use "I." In using passive verbs they also avoid taking responsibility for an action and may, as a result, lessen their credibility:

Passive: Careful consideration *will be given* to the matter.
Active: We will consider the matter carefully.

Passive: *It is recommended* that we accelerate our payments.
Active: I recommend that we accelerate our payments.

While active verbs are preferable to passive verbs, passive verbs do have a few legitimate uses. They may be used as follows:

- *When the doer of an action is unknown or unimportant, that is, when* **what** *was done is more important than* **who** *did it.*
  Kelly was promoted to senior vice-president.
  A cure was found ten years after the virus was identified.

- *When a statement needs to be softened or made impersonal.*
  The policy was disregarded.
  Performance goals were, in many cases, not reached.

- *When a smooth transition from the previous sentence will be achieved.*

Ming Tang was familiar with all relevant export regulations. These regulations had been questioned earlier in the meeting by several committee members.

The samples arrived on the noon plane. They were immediately sent to the laboratory, where Dr. Ryan was waiting.

Using *I*

Although the highly impersonal style that dominated business and government writing has all but vanished, you may still feel uncomfortable using *I*. Yet using *I* ensures clarity and directness, and it adds warmth to a piece of writing.

Use *we* when you are presenting the viewpoint of your firm, but use *I* when you are presenting your own views. Your sentences will sound natural and you'll avoid slipping into passive verbs and awkward constructions:

Passive: It is recommended that we expand our service.
Active: I recommend that we expand our service.

Awkward: The report was written by the undersigned.
Natural: I wrote the report.

After you have drafted a piece of writing, review it to make sure that you haven't overused *I*. You do not want your writing to sound boastful or egocentric. If you fear that you are overusing *I*, try one of these tactics:

- *Move* I *from the beginning of a sentence to the middle:*
  I have been appointed to head the committee and I will be inviting members to speak at these meetings.
  As chairman of the committee, I will be inviting members to speak at these meetings.

- *Refocus a sentence away from yourself and onto the reader:*
  I will send you a list of suggested topics for these talks.
  You will receive a list of suggested topics for these talks.

- *Make a request instead of a statement:*
  I want you to get back to me by next Friday.
  Please respond to me by next Friday.

Tone

When you speak, those listening to you will pick up your tone of voice immediately. They may characterize it as "harsh," "sarcastic," "warm," "condescending," or "sincere," for example." When you write, your readers will also pick up on your tone and will characterize it similarly. Because readers react, and possibly overreact, to the tone of your writing, make sure the tone you convey is the one you intend. Print is permanent.

Though tone is evoked primarily by the words you use, it is also communicated by the amount and kinds of information you present and by the way you structure your message. In reading the following passages, notice that although the ideas are nearly identical, the tone differs significantly.

Passage 1

As a result of someone's carelessness with an ID card, outsiders penetrated our security twice last week and thereby obtained highly confidential materials. Because of this lack of care, we now face the problem of having to issue new ID cards to all holders of blue cards.

If you have a blue card, call Personnel immediately to set up an appointment to get a new one. Once you have it, be sure to follow the rules regarding its use and be more careful in the future. Lost cards seriously threaten our security, and replacing them is expensive.

Passage 2

If you hold a blue ID card, please call Personnel (Ext. 8998) this week to make an appointment to get a new one. Last week unauthorized persons obtained copies of confidential information after gaining entrance to what we thought was our highly secure computer area. Therefore, we are issuing new cards and tightening security.

The new ID cards will be specially coded so that only authorized personnel will be able to enter our high-security areas. When you pick up your new card, its use will be explained. We rely on you to safeguard your card. Since we pride ourselves on our state-of-the-art systems, we must keep them secure at all times.

If the writer of the first passage truly intended to make all the readers (not merely the offenders) feel chastised, he or she certainly succeeded. One asks, however, which memo is more likely to gain the cooperation and foster the goodwill of the employees. When you write, make sure that your tone doesn't work against your getting what you want.

Softening a Negative Message

When you write a negative message, you will want to make sure that it is clear but not unnecessarily harsh. Some of the distinctions below are subtle, indeed, but they may help you come across gracefully and diplomatically. The second sentence in each pair of sentences below is preferable to the first.

State what you can do instead of what you cannot do. Your readers may be more receptive to your ideas if you phrase them positively.

We cannot set up a meeting before May 15.
We can set up a meeting any time after May 15.

We will not process your order until you send payment.
We will process your order as soon as we receive payment.

Replace words that carry strong negative connotations. Some words, like *problems, mixed up, wrong,* and *lazy,* carry negative connotations. If you get rid of these words (unless you are purposely using them for emphasis), your tone will be more positive.

If you have any problems, please call me.
If you have any questions, please call me.

You sent in the wrong form.
We received Form A but need Form B to complete the transaction.

Depersonalize negative statements. Often you can temper your tone by shifting emphasis away from the person's action to the situation, or by shifting the point of view from *you* to *we.*

Your desk is always messy.
Because visitors see your desk when they enter the reception area, please try to keep it neat.

You will not be entitled to interest because you sent in your deposit after the 10th of the month.
Unfortunately we can pay interest only on deposits made by the 10th of the month.

Using passive verbs (normally to be avoided) can also make statements impersonal:

You did not send in your application before the deadline.
Your application was received after the deadline.

6

The Politics of Business Writing

Office Politics and Interoffice Correspondence

A simple memo can cause tongues to wag, ears to burn, eyebrows to raise, and noses to be out of joint. It might even cause heads to roll. The interoffice memo is a powerful document.

Some offices are more political than others, but all operate according to certain unspoken rules. While the political environment and the rules of etiquette differ from company to company, the following general warnings may help you save your neck.

Know when not to write. Highly sensitive or highly personal messages are often better communicated "off the record." Information that is confidential or critical, bombastic or sarcastic should probably not be written either.

Send your memo to the right person. Send your memo to the person responsible for an activity or function. Never go over anyone's head. If you get no results, courtesy demands that you tell the person that you plan to take the matter up with someone in higher authority.

Ask "who" should sign a memo. Occasionally, even though you have written a memo, your boss might want to sign it. If you guess this might be the case, simply ask "Would you like to sign this memo, or should I?"

Send copies to the right people. Send a copy to anyone affected by or interested in the subject, anyone in a direct line of authority between you and the addressee, and anyone you have mentioned in your memo. Avoid sending copies to curry favor or to put someone on the spot.

Avoid turf battles. Concern yourself with issues that fall within your area of responsibility. If you are writing about an issue that involves others, or that others might see as their bailiwick, acknowledge their involvement, compliment them for their contributions, or invite them to collaborate in writing the memo.

Avoid surprising your reader. Prepare your reader for news that might be surprising, especially if the news will not be greeted with enthusiasm. Call ahead to say "You'll be getting a memo later today explaining why we have had to cut your budget," or attach a short covering note that softens the blow.

Give important information to important people first. If you are disseminating important information, consider sending it a couple of days ahead to important people, that is, to those who would be embarrassed if they did not know about it before others. Not everyone reads mail when it arrives.

Ghostwriting

Until you've made it to the very top of the organization, you'll often be asked to write for someone else's signature. Conversely, as your responsibilities grow, you'll ask others to write for your signature. Understanding the following realities of the process may help you and your partner focus on the project and its successful completion.

Setting realistic expectations. No two people think—or write—the same way. Personalities differ and so do the ways we express ourselves. Thus the person who assigns a project should not expect the ghostwriter to produce a report, letter, or memo in exactly the same manner or style as he or she would. The ghostwriter should, in turn, expect changes to be made, even though the draft represents his or her best effort.

Clarifying the task. The two parties should discuss the project so that they are both clear as to its purpose, scope, and content. While one would hope that the person assigning the task knows what he or she wants, this is not always the case. Thus, the writer needs to ask questions before writing—and sometimes while writing—to ensure that the final product will be effective. Misconceptions about the task can lead to unnecessary work and to bad feelings.

Making the style authentic. The style will be authentic only if the one signing the document adds some personal touches to it. The ghostwriter may try to determine a few characteristics of the other person's style but should not become preoccupied with mimicking it. As long as the writer provides a well-written draft, it is the signer's prerogative to make changes as desired. After all, the final product will bear his or her signature.

Editing Someone Else's Writing

No passion in the world, no love or hate, is equal to the passion to change someone else's draft.

In saying this, H. G. Wells recognized the intensity that overtakes a person when editing someone else's writing. (Rarely does the same intensity carry over to the editing of one's own writing.) Few writers respond well to editors who make copious and thoughtless comments. Editing someone else's writing calls for objectivity, maturity, tact, and compassion. Few interactions demand such diplomacy.

A writer has put time and effort into preparing a piece of writing. In giving it over for editing, the writer is putting his or her ego on the line. When editing, realize, therefore, that your remarks, however well meaning, may make the writer feel threatened. You are, after all, criticizing the person's work. Be gentle. Be balanced. Be specific. And be constructive.

Force yourself to read the draft in its entirety. Sit on your hands (literally) or make sure you have no pen or pencil in your hand. Give the draft a chance before you begin reworking it. When you've read it through, ask what your overall impression is. What are the strong points? What are the weak points? How could it be improved? Only after you've considered your comments carefully should you begin to jot them down.

Your Role and Responsibilities

Your role as editor is to sharpen the message and its impact while making as few changes as possible. This role requires that you look at what has been written from the reader's perspective, making changes or suggestions that will improve the document for that reader. You should make no change unless you can give a good reason for it. Finally, you should resist changing anything just because you would have done it, or said it, differently. In short, you'll have to focus on the document and its effectiveness, not on your preferences.

In reviewing a piece of writing, you'll want to look at big issues as well as smaller ones. Pose questions like these to yourself:

Is the information accurate?
Is the document well organized and visually appealing?
Are the points adequately, but not excessively, developed?
Are paragraphs and sentences easy to read?
Are the language and tone appropriate?
Are grammar, spelling, and punctuation correct?

Use good judgment in responding to what has been written. Keep your comments short. If the piece needs to be heavily edited, talk to the writer about it, expanding on the comments you've jotted down. Explain why you think something needs to be changed and suggest changes you think will improve the piece. Do not rob the writer of self-confidence. Make the writer feel better about what he or she has written because of the changes you've made or suggested. (Admittedly, this is sometimes hard to do.)

Your role as editor is important, for you can look at a piece of writing objectively—something that is difficult, or impossible, for a writer to do. (See "Editing Is a Must" on p. 51.)

Language and Sexual Bias

The issue of gender has become, for many, a political issue. For centuries, masculine pronouns *(he, his, him, himself)* have been used to refer to both sexes. A sentence like "Everyone has been issued his own identification card" was grammatically and socially correct. Business letters that began with the salutation "Dear Sir" were, similarly, correct.

As society and values change, however, so too does the language. The societal changes that have taken place over the last two decades are nowhere more noticeable than in the workplace. Women now comprise nearly 50 percent of the work force. Women hold jobs once held only by men and men now hold jobs that were once held by women. Stereotypes have broken down.

Occupational titles have become gender-neutral. Airline stewards and stewardesses are now referred to as flight attendants. Mailmen and mailwomen are called letter carriers. Firemen and firewomen are called fire fighters. Chairmen and chairwomen are now chairs or chairpersons. "Men Working" signs have been reissued. They now read "Road Work" or "People Working." What once seemed extreme is now becoming commonplace.

No matter what your views on the subject are, when writing for business you must consider your reader's reaction to the language you use. You cannot afford to offend a reader. By referring to women differently from men or by using only masculine nouns and pronouns, you may imply an attitude that you do not intend, an attitude that may be objectionable to male and female readers alike. The following tactics can prevent your excluding or offending a reader.

Treat Both Sexes Equally

If you are writing to a general audience, use "Dear Sir or Madam," instead of "Dear Sir." Better yet, use the title or role of the person to whom you are writing: "Dear Owner," "Dear Sales Manager," "Dear Member," "Dear Customer."

If you use a man's first and last name, use a woman's first and last name. If you use Mr., you should also use Ms. or Mrs. If you do not use Mr., you should not use Ms. or Mrs. If you use titles for men, use comparable titles for women.

Do not give out personal information (marital status, age, physical or personal characteristics) about people of either sex unless the information is relevant.

Eliminate Masculine Pronouns

If you are using a pronoun to refer to people in general or to unspecified individuals, avoid using just masculine pronouns. Our language provides many alternatives:

USE PLURAL NOUNS AND PRONOUNS.
  Each supervisor should inform his staff of the new policy.
  Supervisors should inform their staffs of the new policy.

ELIMINATE THE PRONOUN.
  The boss who does everything himself will soon be overworked.
  The boss who tries to do everything will soon be overworked.

SHIFT TO *YOU.*
  Any employee wishing to change the beneficiary on his insurance policy should contact the Benefits Office.
  If you wish to change the beneficiary on your insurance policy, please contact the Benefits Office.

Whenever the reader can be addressed directly, *you* is preferred. *Caution:* Be careful not to shift back and forth between *you* and *he* or *she*. (See "Shifts in Person" on page 130.)

USE BOTH MASCULINE AND FEMININE PRONOUNS.

A writer should ensure that his style is authentic.

A writer should ensure that his or her style is authentic.

Caution: If this form is overused, it can be distracting. Even more awkward is the use of *s/he* or *he/she*. Used occasionally, *he or she* and *him or her* go unnoticed by readers. Use this option when those mentioned above fail to capture your meaning.

In time, language will adapt to the current social and political realities. One or more of these forms—or some new ones—will emerge as preferred. Meanwhile, these usages may seem a bit strange, but lest a writer offend a reader, he or she should adopt them.

7

Writing for Special Purposes

The Executive Summary

An executive summary is a short (usually one page or less) synopsis of a report. For some readers, the summary previews the report; for others it replaces the full report. Because readers see and read the summary first, it should engage their attention and make a good impression.

Structure

Executive summaries take different forms depending on the nature of the report and on company practices. Whatever the form, the opening sets the context and scope of the report. It reminds readers of why the report was written or why it is significant.

The summary may be organized in one of two ways. The traditional approach sets the context, explains the method of investigation—especially if it is controversial or of great interest to readers—then presents the report's major findings and conclusions. Finally, it states the recommendations. (See the example on page 89.) The second, more direct approach presents the recommendations immediately after the opening, then backs them up. (See the example on page 90.)

Tips for Writing

In writing the executive summary, remember to focus on important information, conclusions, and recommendations. Avoid including excessive background and detail.

One manager who had trouble writing the executive summary discovered a helpful technique: He imagined that he and his boss got on the elevator on the 25th floor and rode down to the lobby. His boss remarked, "I just received your report on the new employee incentive plan. What's it all about?" The manager would—in the time it takes an elevator to descend 25 floors—give his boss the rationale, findings, and recommendations of the report.

Depending on how tall your building is—or how fast or slow the elevators are—you may want to try this technique to help you frame the summary.

EXECUTIVE SUMMARY

At the managers' meeting in June, several managers noted that they were spending a significant and disproportionate amount of time on personnel issues. They felt that most problems stem from an increase in part-time workers and from time lost because of absenteeism. The Human Resources Department agreed to study the problem and recommend solutions.

Methodology

We reviewed employment records for the past decade, comparing our statistics with national norms. We polled managers about their concerns, and we circulated a questionnaire among those hired since 1985 inquiring about their understanding of personnel policies and procedures.

Findings and Conclusions

Our mix of employees has changed over the past four years:

- Part-time employees have increased by 24%.
- Employees with no previous work experience have increased by 15%.
- Women employees have increased by 21%.

The following consequences of these changes have been identified:

- Many employees do not understand our policies and procedures.
- Routine projects take longer to complete because of the involvement of more personnel or less well-trained personnel.

Recommendations

We are willing to take the following actions to help remedy the problem:

- Conduct half-day seminars for managers and their staffs to review policies and procedures.
- Institute orientation and training programs for new employees.
- Explore the possibility of flextime and in-house day care.

EXECUTIVE SUMMARY

Our inability to meet demand for the new Model QT terminal has created long shipping delays for customers. Though production will be increased when the Thompson plant begins shipping terminals in May, we may lose some important clients before then. Consequently, we recommend two short-term measures to ease the shortage.

Recommendations for Easing Shortage of QT Terminals

<u>Substitute Model PT for internal orders.</u> Three hundred Model QTs are on order by internal users. While we do not want to accelerate delivery to outside customers at the expense of our own efficiency, most of the QTs on order internally can be replaced by the Model PT. Where the PT is not suitable, shipment of the QT will be delayed for six or more months.

<u>Route QT parts directly to North Carolina for assembly.</u> Now all QT parts are routed from St. Louis to our warehouse in Delaware. By routing the parts directly to North Carolina we can gain two weeks.

Clear Instructions

At one time or another you may have tried to follow instructions that forced you to throw your hands up in despair. Though seemingly a simple task, writing clear instructions demands careful thought and execution. Every step must be delineated, every doubt clarified, every risk defined. Whether a set of instructions is a formal document that will be included in a procedures manual or an informal note explaining how to get to the new plant, it should be simple and clear.

If you want to perfect the art of writing clear instructions, study the way recipes are written, for they incorporate several sound practices: They list everything needed to perform the task, give steps in proper sequence, describe the actions to be taken, use familiar words, and help cooks know when the intended results have been achieved. The writers of cookbooks realize that they have to step outside their own area of expertise to see a situation from the point of view of a novice.

Follow these ten steps to write good instructions:

1. *Prepare your reader for the task.* Start by defining the task and listing the equipment or materials necessary to perform it. If relevant, include other preliminary remarks that set up the process and describe its purpose or importance.

2. *Use familiar terms.* Remember that the person who needs instructions is unlikely to understand specialized vocabulary. A term like "sysgened configuration" tossed into a basic set of computer instructions should be avoided or, if used, should be defined in language everyone can comprehend.

3. *Adhere strictly to chronological order.* Be sure that the instructions give the steps in the sequence in which they should be performed. The next two sentences in a set of instructions

should obviously be reversed: "Freeze the solution for several hours, or until firm. Before freezing it, make sure that the solution is blended well and that the color is uniform."

4. *Give all necessary warnings.* Explain conditions under which an operation should not be performed: "CAUTION: Do not operate this equipment during electrical storms."

5. *Relate the unknown to the known.* Compare the new task to one that is familiar to the reader: "Grasp the first chopstick like a pencil."

6. *Reassure the reader.* Insert occasional phrases that tell the reader he or she is proceeding correctly: "If you have completed this step properly, the green light will flash when you push the red button."

7. *Explain reasons for performing a step.* Tell your reader why a step is being taken if the explanation will help that person understand the process or complete the step accurately: "Maintain the activity for 20 minutes so that the full aerobic effect will be achieved."

8. *Use an easy-to-follow format.* Number the steps so that the reader will be able to focus on one step at a time and find the next step easily.

9. *Include drawings or diagrams.* Use a visual aid if it will explain something more clearly than words. Ensure that the art work is simple and properly labeled.

10. *Try out the instructions.* Have someone follow the instructions so that you can discover where they are confusing or unclear. Revise the troublesome sections and test your instructions again.

The instructions on pages 94 and 95 from the Kaypro II *User's Guide** are easy to read and easy to follow. Any terminology used has been explained in preceding sections.

**Used with permission of the Kaypro Corporation, which makes no claim as to the accuracy of the material.

FORMATTING A DISKETTE

<u>Before</u> you can store information on a new diskette
(for example, text you want to write with Perfect
Writer, or an S-BASIC program), you must first format
that disk. When you do this, you prepare the disk so
information can be stored on it. If you do not
format a disk, then you won't be able to store
information on it. (Note: During the copy process,
as described previously, the new diskettes in drive B
were automatically formatted before the copying took
place).

When you format a disk, it is magnetically imprinted
with 40 circular tracks, each track having 10
sectors.

Each track is
a concentric
ring.

Each sector is
a pie-shaped
wedge.

Illustration of a disk format

To format a disk, you will call up the BLANK option from the copy program. To do this:

step 1. Turn on or reset the computer.

step 2. Insert the working copy of your CP/M S-BASIC diskette in drive A.

step 3. Type: COPY
Press the RETURN key.

step 4. When the main menu appears, type B to use the BLANK option.

step 5. Read the message on the screen, and place a new diskette in drive B.

step 6. Press the RETURN key.

step 7. Watch the screen to see the formatting track numbers (00 through 39). When the last track is formatted, CP/M will be written to the disk. After this, the main menu will appear again. To exit, type E.

The diskette in drive B has been formatted and is now ready to store information.

Delivering Unwelcome News

It's not easy to be the bearer of unwelcome news, but some writers make the task harder than necessary. They either adopt a false, overapologetic tone that makes the reader feel patronized, or they so mask the message that the reader feels duped. One should not go to the opposite extreme, however, and become blunt, unfeeling, or brutal.

Bad news is a fact of everyday business life. Businessmen and -women are usually mature enough to want it straight. They also want reasons for the news. They even want a little humanity in the way thay are given the news.

Sometimes you may find it easier to communicate the news in person or on the phone, for you can easily soften the message with your tone of voice. A spoken message may also come across with less authority and finality than a written message.

When you do write, avoid sandwiching the bad news between an irrelevant, indirect, or overly cushioned beginning and end. Avoid overstating your sorrow. Avoid making upbeat statements that attempt to force goodwill on the reader who is really not in the mood to be a jolly-good sport.

In most cases you can do the following:

- State the context.
- Tell the reader the unwelcome news.
- Give specific reasons for your denial.
- Offer alternatives or encouragement, if appropriate.
- End courteously.

See pages 97 and 98 for examples of this type of letter.

MACE, DEERING, KLINGER & SMITH
5525 Thornridge Park
Cambridge, MA 02140
876-9898

March 3, 1989

Ms. Catherine Coombs
12 Elm Street
Cambridge, MA 02139

Dear Ms. Coombs:

Thank you for contacting us about getting your unit exempted from rent control. Based upon the information you provided, your unit does not qualify for exemption, according to the requirements set by the Rent Control Board.

Two reasons prevent your unit from qualifying: Your walls were not taken down to the studs before they were rebuilt, and your boiler predates 1969.

Thus, if you want to rent your condominium, you will have to charge the rent stipulated by the Rent Control Board.

Please call if I can be of further help.

Sincerely,

Gail Flynn-Lanska

Gail Flynn-Lanska
Senior Associate

NEW YORK UNIVERSITY
SCHOOL OF LAW

Committee on Admissions
40 Washington Square South, New York, New York 10012

March 14, 1989

Jane Doe
875 West End Avenue
New York, NY 10025

Dear Ms. Doe:

The Committee on Admissions has carefully considered your application and I am sorry to report that we are unable to offer you admission to the School of Law. Approximately 6,500 candidates are competing for admission this year, which means that the Committee has been required to make many difficult choices.

We hope that you understand that our decision on your application is not an estimate of your potential as a law student or an attorney. Since the vast majority of our applicants are clearly capable of success in law school and beyond, we inevitably must turn away many who we know will succeed in law simply for lack of space in our class.

Please accept our best wishes for your future educational and career plans.

Sincerely,

Nan McNamara
Assistant Dean
for Admissions

NMcN/wej

A private university in the public service

This form letter is used with the author's permission.

98

Letters of Complaint

When you're dissatisfied with products, services, and policies, *do* take the time to put your complaint in writing. Not only does a letter force the recipient to deal with the issue, but it also forces you to deal with your concern logically and completely.

Complaint letters are easy to write, though controlling your emotions is not so easy. Since an angry or scolding tone may work against you, attempt to empty yourself of your ugliest feelings before sitting down to write.

The letter should be simple and firm. After identifying the purpose for your writing, you need to cover three basic points:

The problem—what happened or didn't happen.
The cost—in terms of inconvenience, aggravation, or money.
The solution—the remedy you suggest.

You must, of course, supply adequate details so that the reader can fully understand the situation. Dates, places, times, names of people involved, and pertinent numbers (purchase order, invoice, or model) are among the facts you should include.

In an initial complaint, at least, it pays to assume goodwill on the part of the organization you are dealing with and to expect that it will wish to rectify the situation. Most companies willingly correct what went wrong or, if that is impossible, explain why the situation occurred.

The letter on the next page uses the approach recommended. While the letter shows displeasure, it focuses on the facts:

January 8, 1989

Alphonse Geller
Ace Service Company
300 Wilson Boulevard
Atlanta, GA 30346

Dear Mr. Geller:

We were recently overcharged by your company for repairs made to three of our copy machines.

On November 30, 1988, Mr. Eng of your firm visited our plant in Three Oaks to estimate the cost of overhauling our copy machines. According to him, three of our machines required servicing at a cost of $100 to $150 each, depending on how many parts needed replacement.

On January 5, 1989, Mr. Sakey and Mr. Cruz repaired the machines and left a bill for $629 (copy enclosed). This bill exceeds your maximum estimate by $179.

A call to Mr. Eng on January 6 gave us little satisfaction. He said that the costs were higher than estimated because the work took longer than expected. But according to the estimate, the cost depended on the number of parts needing replacement, not on the time spent at our plant.

Please issue us a revised bill that is in line with your original estimate. Please also itemize the bill to show the repairs made to, and the parts replaced on, each machine.

Sincerely,

Arthur L. Rubino

Arthur L. Rubino
Plant Manager

Enclosure

Responses to Letters of Complaint

People who take the time to write letters of complaint are entitled to a courteous and prompt reply. No matter whether the complaint is justified or not, you should answer in a responsible, professional way. Never trivialize the situation or belittle your reader, even if he or she seems to be a grumbler.

In answering complaints, you should do four things: acknowledge, explain, reassure, and apologize.

Acknowledge. First, acknowledge that the person has a right to complain. If the complaint is justified, you can begin your letter at once by stating that the customer is right: "Your records are correct. We overstated your tax bill by $212.00." If, on the other hand, the complaint is unjustified, you can, at the very least, thank the customer for having brought the matter to your attention: "Thank you for taking the time to let us know about your experiences using our product."

Explain. Find out what happened and explain it. A person rarely tires of reading a response to his or her complaint. And by taking the time to explain thoroughly what happened, you come across as being concerned and conscientious. Avoid citing company policy to explain why something did or did not happen, unless you explain why that policy is necessary. If your explanation involves admitting that your company was wrong, consult your legal department. Issues involving liability can be tricky.

Reassure. Quickly, but sincerely, let your reader know that the situation has been, or is being, resolved. Avoid saying that the problem will not recur unless you are sure it will not.

Apologize. Say you are sorry for the person's trouble, inconvenience, or frustration.

People are usually reasonable, especially if you have been sincere and honest. Well-worded responses can win back your reader's loyalty and restore the goodwill felt toward you and your company.

Sidney Susskind, sales manager for Computer Warehouse, received the letter of complaint on the opposite page. His response follows on page 104.

Claremont Road
Pittsburgh, PA 15250
February 7, 1989

Sidney Susskind
Sales Manager
Computer Warehouse
1200 Creighton Boulevard
Pittsburgh, PA 15250

Dear Mr. Susskind:

I am writing to express my dissatisfaction at the treatment I received in your store last week.

While attempting to return a software package, I was treated rudely and was refused a refund by your employee, John Cabriol. He insinuated that I had copied the disk and was returning it for a refund. In point of fact, it was not until I had opened the package that I realized the software was not compatible with my computer.

I have done business with your store for years but will not patronize it again. I do not like to be treated disrespectfully nor do I like to do business with stores that have unreasonable return policies.

Sincerely,

Hugo Channing
Hugo Channing

1200 Creighton Boulevard   Pittsburgh, PA 15250
576-9300

February 17, 1989

Hugo Channing
Claremont Road
Pittsburgh, PA 15250

Dear Mr. Channing:

Thank you for letting us know about the situation that occurred in our store last week. I agree that the salesperson who waited on you should have been more courteous. Mr. Cabriol has been reprimanded. I apologize for any embarassment he may have caused you.

I am sorry that you were not fully aware of our policy on returning computer software when you made your purchase. We do our best to advertise the policy widely. Once a package has been opened, we cannot resell it; customers think that the software has been used or that it is defective.

We believe that our policy is reasonable and hope you can appreciate why we have such a policy. We can offer wholesale prices only because we keep our overhead low and our services to a minimum.

We do value your patronage and hope you will reconsider doing business with us again. I will be pleased to offer you an additional 10% discount on any software in stock and have enclosed a letter authorizing this discount.

Sincerely,

Sidney Susskind

Sidney Susskind
Sales Manager

Enclosure

Letters of Recommendation

Letters of recommendation usually follow a useful, well-established form. In writing one, you should do the following:

- State the name of the person and the role or position you are recommending the person for.
- Explain how long and in what capacity you have known the person.
- Identify the individual's skills, knowledge, experience, or work habits. (Consider what information the recipient of the letter will find helpful.)
- Mention a couple of qualities that make the individual special.
- Reiterate your recommendation.

Depending on how well you know the person you are recommending, how enthusiastic you are about recommending him or her, and whom the letter is going to, you may want to reorganize the parts or develop some portions in greater (or lesser) detail.

Be as specific as possible. If you state that someone "takes initiative and follows through," provide substantiation: "When Claudia realized that the department would be converting to flextime, she polled employees as to their preferences, worked out a schedule, presented it for approval, and then introduced the program to employees."

Striking the right tone is difficult. You need to sound enthusiastic without being gushy. Too many superlatives lend a note of insincerity. Above all, maintain a balance between your desire to help a deserving individual and your obligation to maintain the integrity of your profession or organization, and your own good name.

Turn the page for an example of a letter of recommendation.

RALLY CORPORATION

May 1, 1989

Ms. Mary Louise Clare
Executive Vice President
Expert Systems, Inc.
6678 Avenue B
Albany, NY 12205

Dear Ms. Clare:

I'm pleased to recommend William MacMillan as a Design Consultant for your firm. Bill totally renovated three plants for us over the last five years. He is now working on a fourth plant.

We had a special interest in hiring Bill because of his reputation for retaining the architectural integrity of old, yet well-designed, buildings. He deserves the reputation he has earned. Our plants have been featured in several architectural magazines. The buildings are not only beautiful; they are also functional. By adding a loft, he expanded the useable space in each plant by nearly 20%.

Bill remains involved in a project from start to finish. He oversees the construction and keeps management informed about its progress. He's proud of his work and likes to drive by "just to see how it's coming along."

In my opinion you could do no better than to hire Bill. Give me a call if I can answer any questions, and do feel free to come by and see the fine work he's done for us.

Sincerely,

Richard A. Linskey

Richard A. Linskey
Vice President
Buildings and Grounds

KELLY ROAD
ALBANY, NY 12207
(518) 795-9500

Thank-You Notes

The most important thing about a thank-you note is the fact that you've taken the time to write it. People scarcely remember what you say in the note, but they do remember that you've sent it.

A thank-you note should be short. (Try double-spacing it or using smaller stationery.)

- Say "thank you" and indicate what you are saying thanks for.
- Mention how you, or others, benefited—overall and specifically.
- Look forward to another opportunity to interact with the person.

You needn't be clever, but you should be sincere.

Thank-you notes like the examples on pages 108 and 109 take just a few minutes to write but they go a long way toward making people feel good about themselves and about you.

December 1, 1988

Jill Sullivan
Chemicals Plus
12 Wheeler Street
Boston, MA 02125

Dear Jill,

Thank you for addressing our group last Friday. My staff enjoyed your talk so much that they have asked me to invite you back. That, you should know, is a real compliment.

We especially appreciated your covering issues related to product safety. In the past, many of us have skirted the issue with clients. Now we'll be able to sell our product knowing that its chemicals are less harmful than the chemicals in our drinking water.

Can we book you to speak at our meeting in May?

Sincerely,

Frank

Francis P. Otto
Regional Sales Manager

October 12, 1988

To: Kenneth McAllister
From: James D. Olivieri
Re: Appreciation

Thank you for your hard work, and for your calm confidence these last few weeks. While we were all jumping off desks and complaining about the client, you were working away diligently, knowing, somehow, that we'd meet the deadline. You're a real asset to the department.

Remind me to buy you lunch—once I start taking lunch hours again.

Memos "To File"

By writing "to file," you can record information you might forget at a later date. In the current business environment, writing to file also serves other purposes. It allows you to establish your involvement in an issue, claim ownership of an idea, or protect your position or status.

When you write a memo to file, keep it short, but make sure it is not so cryptic that you will not understand it months later.

The example on the opposite page is one such memo.

MEMO TO FILE

Date: April 2, 1989   Subject: "SMILE" as Concentrate

Phone Call to: Sandy Peters

Purpose: To let him know I'm against marketing a concentrate.

Issues Raised: 1) Consumers don't want to mix product. Messy and time consuming.
2) Product may not taste the same. Inexact measuring may result in over- or under-dilution.
3) Sticker price for 12 oz. of concentrate is higher than for 12 oz. of pre-mixed product. Even though 12 oz. of concentrate yields 24 oz. of mouthwash, customer may not calculate the difference in price.

Reactions: Sandy still wants to go ahead. He will talk to product manager first, he says.

D.P.
Denise Pullen

Persuasion: Some Practical Pointers

Persuading another person to your point of view is a difficult—but not impossible—task. You will, of course, have to present solid facts and logical arguments to win over your reader, but before deciding on what facts you'll use, step back and assess your chances of success. Then, once you have a realistic idea of your potential to succeed, plan a strategy that incorporates some common sense. Do not get so carried away with developing evidence for your case that you forget the more human aspects of persuasion.

Assess Your Chances of Success

Your chance of succeeding will improve if you take the time to analyze three variables—your reader's readiness to accept your position, his or her bias toward your position, and his or her attitude toward you.

Reader readiness. Readers act only when they are ready to; thus, part of your task will be to bring your reader to the point where he or she can comfortably say "yes." In some cases your reader may have insufficient knowledge about an issue. Before you launch into strong arguments in favor of your position, you will have to step back and inform that person of the importance of the issue. You can then proceed to presenting evidence in favor of your position. In another case your reader may consider an issue important but, because of other limitations or priorities, is not ready to hear your case. You'll have to delay your appeal or show your reader why your issue demands immediate attention.

Reader bias. Assess also your reader's position on the issue. If he or she is favorably inclined, develop a few strong reasons and focus on motivating action. If your reader is neutral, give your best arguments. Be sure you are objective, practical, and moderate. If your reader is negatively inclined, be especially sure that your reasoning is airtight and your evidence sound. If your reader is able to poke holes in your arguments, you will lose your case. Try to discover the reasons for the person's bias. They may give you some clues for alternative approaches.

Reader attitude. If your reader thinks you are highly credible, you stand a good chance of convincing him or her—all other factors being equal. If your credibility is unestablished or low, rely heavily on developing strong factual evidence. Consider having someone else sign your document—someone who has higher credibility, of course—or get others whom your reader respects to buy into your idea first. You will, in this case, borrow credibility to help you convince your reader.

Use Some Common Sense

Facts alone rarely convince. Facts, together with an approach sensitive to your reader's human and psychological needs, will more likely convince. Try always to establish some common ground before presenting your argumentative appeals so that your reader will be in a receptive frame of mind. Throughout the persuasive appeal, practice three virtues: patience, prudence, and flexibility.

Patience. Seldom will you persuade your reader in a single attempt. The process can take time and multiple attempts. Some may be written, some oral, some formal, some informal. Courting your reader demands patience.

Prudence. Be careful not to push your ideas too hard—especially if your reader is not immediately taken with them. If your pursuit is unrelenting, your reader might become recalcitrant. Be careful, too, not to make promises you can't keep, and don't exaggerate. If you inflate just one fact or figure, and your reader realizes it, he or she will question other assertions as well.

Flexibility. When you realize you may not get all of what you want, you may have to make a few concessions. Don't give in too soon and weaken your case, but don't hold out for everything. You may get nothing. Keep an open dialogue with the person you are trying to convince. By determining the sticking points, you may be able to modify your approach and end up getting some of what you want—if some is better than none to you.

Shaping a Persuasive Message

Attempts to analyze how man thinks and acts date back to the time of Aristotle. Within our own century, various dynamic theories of persuasion have been advanced. One of these theories, the "motivated sequence," applies well to business because it focuses on the psychological needs of the reader. First presented by Alan H. Monroe and D. Ehninger, the motivated sequence consists of five steps: attention, need, satisfaction, visualization, and action.* Because these steps follow the normal thought process, Monroe hypothesized that using them to organize a message motivates the receiver to respond.

Attention. Before a reader can be persuaded, his or her attention must be engaged. You can use a standard attention-getting device such as a promise of greater profitability, productivity,

*A. H. Monroe and D. Ehninger, *Principles of Speech Communication*, 7th brief ed. (Glenville, Ill.: Scott Foresman and Co., 1975), pp. 241–262.

efficiency, improved morale or status—anything, in short, that will seize the reader's interest.

Need. Once you've captured the reader's attention, state that a need or problem exists. Reinforce and dramatize the need by providing examples and details.

Satisfaction. Having established a need, develop your proposal and show how it meets that need. Anticipate the reader's questions and objections, show the adequacy and advantages of your solution, and, if necessary, discuss alternative solutions to show that you have been thorough and objective.

Visualization. Then intensify the reader's desire to accept your plan by describing exactly how it will work.

Action. Tell your reader what you want him or her to do. Enlisting your reader's assistance will help him or her become committed to your plan.

In order to persuade, you must stimulate, inform, and activate the reader. Other variables, like the significance of the issue, the bias of the reader, and your credibility, must also be considered, for no formula will work in and of itself. The writer of the memo on pages 116–17 and her boss share a good working relationship in an efficient, cost-effective department. The boss is generally slow to accept change and needs to be led through a sequence of justifications before being convinced.

To: Robert McDougall, Vice President of Marketing

From: Janet M. Fischer, Assistant Vice-President *JMF*

Re: Purchasing a Personal Computer for Marketing

- -

Considerable savings will be achieved, both in time and money, if we buy a personal computer (PC) for our department.

Our present dependence on the company's mainframe system is unsatisfactory in several respects:

- The mainframe excels in complicated number crunching. Using the mainframe for our relatively simple needs is not a sound application of company resources.

- The mainframe is tied up 75% of the time, leaving non-prime hours for us. As a result, we often resort to overtime to complete our projects.

- The word-processing add-on to the mainframe is inadequate for turning out our reports. It is cumbersome and does not produce professional-looking copy.

- The language and commands of the system are unnecessarily difficult; thus many staff members do not use the system, continuing instead to perform operations manually.

Having our own PC would decrease costs and increase productivity:

<u>An 80% Decrease in Costs.</u> We would avoid the computer department's hourly charges ($10-$15), and we could complete most of our work from 9 to 5, thus eliminating most overtime costs. Last year we paid out about $5,500 to the computer department and $2,500 in overtime—a total of $8,000.

<u>An Increase in Productivity.</u> Specialized software would permit us to calculate our trend analyses and forecasts more efficiently. A more powerful word-processing component would allow our staff to write, store, and edit reports quickly and easily. Once staff members became comfortable with a "friendly" computer, they would use it for additional applications. I estimate a 20% increase in productivity within six months.

Jack Sadowski bought a PC for the Purchasing Department last year. He estimates that we could buy a computer, three or four software packages, and a quality printer for about $4,000 - $6,000. Hiring a person to train our staff and help us develop our own programs could run another $2,000. Taking a top dollar of $8,000, we would be looking at a one-year payback. But if we depreciate the equipment over five years, **our cost for the equipment would be only $1,200—one-fifth of our present computer costs.** (Vinnie Mercado will have a detailed cost estimate ready next week.)

In short, by spending less we can computerize more tasks and get them done more quickly. Staff will also work more willingly and more productively. If we purchase the PC and train staff by the end of April, we can be fully operational before our busiest time of year.

Patti, Keith, and I would be pleased to explore the issue further—and Jack will offer advice as needed. Suzanne tells me you are free next Wednesday afternoon. I'll drop by your office then to discuss my plan with you. Please call me if you have any questions before then.

Messages for Electronic Mail

Electronic mail (E-Mail) systems turn computer terminals into in-boxes. The system may be used to transmit lengthy documents inside or outside the company but is most often used to transmit short messages—usually those that require a quick response.

In writing messages that require a quick response, you can depart from many common writing conventions, but make sure that the speed the technology provides does not cause you to become careless. Veteran users of electronic mail offer the following suggestions and cautions to neophytes:

Write an informative subject line. Phrase the subject line so that it tells the reader *what to do* instead of, or in addition to, what the memo is about. A subject line may read: "Urgent: Get year-end figures to Joe," or "Proceed with distribution of vaccine." A precise subject line can prompt a reader to read your message before others.

Keep screen length in mind when organizing. Organize your message so that the most important information fits on the first screen. Remember, if your message goes onto a second or third screen, earlier screens are no longer visible to your reader. Avoid long messages.

Make it easy for your reader to respond. Word a message so that the reader can get back with a "yes/no" answer or a short response. Where possible, use questions instead of statements. Instead of saying "Let me know your thoughts on Cory's proposal," ask "Should we adopt Cory's proposal?"

Be concise. Use phrases or sentences, short words, and abbreviations, but be careful that your message is not so cryptic that it must be decoded or so terse that it seems rude. Make sure too that your style is not so disjointed or casual that you would be embarrassed if your message were read by a wide audience.

Don't forget that many people may read your message. Just like regular correspondence, E-Mail can be forwarded by the receiver (by the push of a button) or printed out and distributed to others. Make sure that the message shows you at your best.

Don't be too quick to push the "Send" button. Think seriously about what you've written, and the reaction it is likely to produce, *before* you send a message. Unlike regular correspondence that can easily be retrieved from the out-box or the mail room, E-Mail cannot be recovered without the assistance of a programmer.

Don't send highly confidential messages. Every message is backed up and stored on tape. Even if you delete a message, it is not erased from the system's memory. (Oliver North did not realize this.) By virtue of their job responsibilities, the staff maintaining the system also has access to all files. Thus, nothing is truly secret.

A Glossary of Grammar and Usage

Your grammar and usage should be correct for two reasons—clarity and credibility. An ungrammatical sentence or a misused word can confuse or distract your readers and can cause you to look bad. Like bad manners, bad grammar and usage reflect your background and educational level. Mistakes can lessen the opinion your readers hold of you and can lead them to question your expertise in other matters. For the most part, your grammar and usage will go unnoticed—until you make a mistake, that is.

Following the rules of grammar facilitates understanding. Everyone agrees that the meanings of "The dog bit the man" and "The man bit the dog" are different. Because grammar rules are fixed, meaning is fixed.

Similarly, standards for usage, the way words are used, ensure that meaning is shared. If your readers don't know exactly what you mean by a word, clarity will be lost.

The following glossary explains points of grammar and usage that perplex many business writers.

a, an

The use of *a* or *an* is dictated not by the first letter of the word that follows but by its initial sound. *A* precedes words beginning with consonant sounds (a meeting, a proposal). *An* precedes words beginning with vowel sounds (an announcement, an itinerary). Thus *a historian, a utility,* and *a one-year lease* are correct. The words following the article begin with consonant sounds—*h, y,* and *w. An honorable occasion, an NBC reporter,* and *an $80,000 salary* are correct because the sounds immediately following the articles are vowel sounds—*on, en,* and *a.*

abbreviations

- Abbreviate titles when they precede or follow names but not when they appear without a name:

Lt. Col. Daniels   Harold Remmer, M.D.   Carolyn Conroy, Ph.D.
Mr. Michael Quinn   Ms. Lillian Goodhue

The lieutenant colonel was honored at a testimonial dinner.
The doctor prescribed two aspirin and a good night's sleep.

- Abbreviate names of organizations, governmental agencies, companies, and some common terms. Periods are not generally used:

PTA   AFL-CIO   FBI   IBM   AT&T   GNP   AWOL   ID

(Abbreviations that are pronounced as words—NOW, HUD, NATO, WASP—are called acronyms.)

If your reader might be unfamiliar with an abbreviation or acronym, identify it the first time you use it. Put either the abbreviation or the unabbreviated form in parentheses:

The company grants a Cost of Living Adjustment (COLA) each year.
An ATM (Automatic Teller Machine) will be installed in the lobby.

- Use the abbreviations *Co., Bros., Corp.,* and *Inc.* and the ampersand (&) with the name of the firm if the abbreviation is part of the official name of the company. Write the word out if you are using it without the name:

Harper & Row, Publishers, Inc.   Aberdeen Co., Inc.
but Boston Edison Company   The Forum Corporation

The company is expanding into new markets.

- Avoid abbreviating months of the year, days of the week, cities, and the words *street, road,* or *avenue.* Abbreviate the names of states (use the two-letter abbreviations designated by the U.S. Postal Service) in addresses, but not within sentences.

He will be moving to Warren, Michigan, in August. His address there will be 3462 Bedford Road
         Warren, MI 48089.

- Avoid using Latin abbreviations such as *i.e., e.g., viz.* Substitute English phrases *(that is, for example, namely).*

affect, effect

Affect, a verb, refers to an action. It is interchangeable with *change* or *influence:*

The resignation of a veteran employee *affects* [changes] the unit's operation in several ways.
The strike will *affect* [influence] shipments.
The president's announcement *affected* [influenced] us profoundly.

Effect, a noun, is interchangeable with *a result* or *the result:*

The resignation of a veteran employee has a number of *effects* [results] upon the unit's operation.
What will the *effects* [results] of the strike be?
The *effect* [result] of the president's announcement was startling.

The verb *to effect,* meaning *to bring about* or *to put into effect,* can be replaced by the verb *to make.* In fact, using *make* is preferable; *to effect* is a bit stilted.

We will *effect* [bring about] this change as of the first of the year.
We will *make* this change as of the first of the year.

and, beginning sentences with

There is no basis for objecting to *and*—or any other word—at the beginning of a sentence. But sentences beginning with *and* should not be overused. They can be especially effective toward the end of a paragraph, after several other points have been made. They can change the pace of a series of sentences. And they can add emphasis by forcing the reader to pause between two statements rather than run them together.

bad/badly

Both "I feel bad" and "I feel badly" are correct, depending on what you mean. "I feel bad" means "I'm sorry," or "I'm not well." "I feel badly" means "My sense of touch is impaired."

> I feel bad because my raise didn't come through.
> My boss feels bad for me, too.

Both sentences are correct.

Confusion sets in because *badly* is used correctly in such sentences as "Alfred has never spoken badly of you" and "The last shipment arrived badly damaged." But *bad* follows certain verbs of sense—that is, *feel, look, taste, smell.* Thus the following sentences are also correct:

> The last catalogue looked bad. The printing was smudged.
> This cream cheese tastes bad, but the bagel tastes good.
> The office smelled bad because he had just smoked a cheap cigar.

comma splice

A comma splice occurs when a writer joins two sentences with a comma. What looks simply like an error in punctuation really constitutes an error in grammar. These sentences are *incorrect:*

> The audit was completed in June, thus the report should be out soon.
> These results are poor, however profits should rebound next year.

The comma splice is easy to correct. In the examples above, the sentences were joined by *thus* or *however*. These words and others like them *(nevertheless, consequently, furthermore, therefore, moreover . . .)* are called conjunctive adverbs. When a conjunctive adverb is used as a transition between two ideas, a period or semicolon (semicolons are more common) separates the two thoughts, and a comma follows the conjunctive adverb.

> The audit was completed in June. Thus, the report should be out soon.
> These results are poor; however, profits should rebound next year.

Coordinating conjunctions *(and, but, or, for, nor),* with commas before them, may also be used to join sentences:

> These results are poor, but profits should rebound next year.
> Costs increased only slightly, and the profit margin remained stable.

Yet another, and often preferable, way to eliminate the comma splice is to recast the ideas by subordinating one idea to the other. By doing this, the relationship between ideas is more accurately expressed:

> Although these results are poor, profits should rebound next year.
> Because costs increased only slightly, the profit margin remained stable.

contractions

Style in business writing has relaxed considerably in the last decade. In many cases contractions are preferred since they sound natural. Listen to your writing. Hear how it sounds. Don't use so many contractions that they call attention to themselves, but don't avoid using them altogether except, perhaps, in a very formal document.

dangling participles

Participles end in *-ing, -en,* or *-ed.* Participial phrases begin with a participle:

Knowing little about finance, . . .
Taken literally, . . .
Viewed from management's perspective, . . .

They dangle when the noun or pronoun after the introductory phrase does not follow logically from the phrase:

Incorrect: Knowing little about finance, the numbers confused me.

The sentence above suggests that "the numbers" knew little about finance. Dangling participles can confuse or amuse your reader.

To correct a dangling participle, make sure that *the first word* after the participial phrase relates to the information given in that introductory phrase:

Correct: Knowing little about finance, *I* was confused by the numbers.

If the sentence sounds awkward, revise it yet again:

Because I knew little about finance, I was confused by the numbers.

Incorrect: Taken literally, we find the regulations quite strict.
Correct: Taken literally, *the regulations* seem quite strict.

Incorrect: Viewed from management's perspective, you might see the situation differently.
Correct: Viewed from management's perspective, *the situation* might seem quite different. *OR* If you view the situation from management's perspective, you might see it differently.

data

Data is the Latin plural form of *datum*. In technical or scholarly writing, *data* is generally used as a plural: "The data were correct." In most business situations, however, *data* is used as a singular collective noun: "The data was correct."

fewer, less

The sign at the checkout counter in the supermarket reads "Less than ten items." It should read "Fewer than ten items."

Fewer refers to number and indicates "how many." It is used with plural nouns: *fewer dollars, fewer machines, fewer conflicts.* *Less* refers to amount and indicates "how much." It is used with singular nouns: *less money, less equipment, less conflict.*

if it was, if it were

The subjunctive form *were* is still used to express hypothetical, doubtful, or contrary-to-fact statements. *Were* is required in the following:

> If the company *were* to relocate . . .
> Assume your company *were* to go bankrupt . . .
> If a discounted rate *were* available . . .

More and more, *was* is used conversationally in such expressions as "If the company was to relocate, most employees would move." Such usage should be confined to informal speech. You may choose to say *was* in the sentence quoted above during a coffee break, but when you return to your desk to write, use *were.*

its, it's

It's (with an apostrophe) should be used only as a contraction for *it is.* Yet, surprisingly, many educated writers consistently misuse *it's* to indicate possession. *Its* is possessive, just like the words *his, hers,* and *ours* (all without apostrophes).

Note the correct use of the two words in the following passage:

> The company announced that *its* profits in the last quarter had exceeded expectations. As a result *its* dividend would be increased by four cents. "*It's* our intention to pass this earnings increase on to stockholders," the company president remarked.

me, myself, I

Most of the errors in the use of *me, myself,* and *I* result from an unconscious but widespread misconception that using *I* is unacceptable in business writing or from the equally false notion that *me* is somehow inelegant and should therefore be avoided. *Myself* becomes the all-purpose substitute.

Incorrect: Bob Ames and myself will continue to service your account.

Correct: Bob Ames and I will continue to service your account.

Incorrect: Call Bob or myself if you have any questions.

Correct: Call Bob or me if you have any questions.

If you are unsure of the correct usage of *me* or *I* in these cases, simply leave the other person out of the sentence and see which of the pronouns occurs naturally. Thus, you would say, "*I* will continue to service your account." When adding Bob to the sentence, keep the same pronoun, *I.* Similarly, "Call *me* if you have any questions." When adding Bob to the sentence, retain *me.*

Myself is used correctly as a reflexive pronoun or as an emphatic device. A reflexive pronoun shows that the doer and receiver of an action are the same: "I hurt myself." When used for emphasis *myself* is interchangeable with "personally," as in "I myself would never have done that."

numbers

Conventionally, numbers one through ten are written out as words. Numbers over ten are written as figures.

Some exceptions apply:

- Use figures to refer to dates, addresses, time of day (except if the word *o'clock* is used), money, decimals, fractions, page and footnote numbers, or phone numbers.
- Use a figure-word combination when referring to large round numbers: 15 million inhabitants, a $12 billion deficit.

- When several numbers appear in the same paragraph, use the same form for consistency. (Figures, because they are quicker to read, are preferable.)
- When a figure begins a sentence, write the figure as a word or rephrase the sentence so that the figure does not appear at the beginning.

Using the number twice, as in "Please sign the two (2) forms," is unnecessary and pretentious. Numbers are repeated in bank checks and in legal contracts to ensure legibility and accuracy and to prevent forgery. Even the *U.S. Government Printing Office Style Manual* (1973) states that a spelled-out number should not be repeated in figures, except in legal contracts.

only

Only is often misplaced in sentences. One reason for its misplacement is the long oral tradition of placing *only* before the verb. Hence, sentences like the following sound natural:

He *only* sent the package yesterday.
We will *only* start the program if everyone approves it.

A reader generally interprets these sentences correctly, even though they could have meanings quite different from those intended. The first sentence could mean "Only he (no one else) sent the package" or "He didn't do anything yesterday but send the package." The second sentence could mean "If everyone approves the program, the only thing we'll do is start it."

By placing *only* as close as possible to what it modifies, you will not risk misinterpretation on the part of your reader.

When rewritten, the above sentences become precise, unambiguous, and correct:

He sent the package *only* yesterday.
We will start the program *only* if everyone approves it.

parallelism

Parallelism is the use of grammatically balanced forms to express two or more ideas of equal weight. Most writers can easily identify simple errors in parallelism. They would have little difficulty revising the following awkward sentence:

Incorrect: I like to figure out a problem and solving it.
Correct: I like to figure out a problem and solve it.

Lack of parallelism is harder to spot in more complicated constructions. It occurs most often in these grammatical situations:

• Where ideas are listed in a series:

Incorrect: The proposal was practical, reasonable in cost, and presented convincingly.
Correct: The proposal was practical, economical, and convincing.

Incorrect: The recommendations should be reviewed by vice-presidents, branch managers, and all who supervise.
Correct: The recommendations should be reviewed by vice-presidents, branch managers, and all supervisors.

• Where ideas are connected by correlatives such as *either . . . or, neither . . . nor, not only . . . but also:*

Incorrect: Neither an increase in sales nor reducing the work force can solve the company's financial woes.
Correct: Neither increasing sales nor reducing the work force will solve the company's financial woes.

Incorrect: The provost was respected not only for her hard work and dedication, but also because she got along well with people.
Correct: The provost was respected not only for her hard work and dedication, but also for her ability to get along well with people.

prepositions, ending sentences with

Winston Churchill is widely credited with having had the last word on this matter. When he was criticized for having ended a sentence with a preposition, he pencilled on a manuscript, "This is the type of arrant pedantry up with which I will not put."

H. W. Fowler, whose *Dictionary of Modern English Usage* (Oxford University Press, 1965) has long been recognized as the Bible in its field, labeled the idea that a preposition must not be used at the end of a sentence a "cherished superstition." These "notions of correctness," Fowler says, derived from Latin standards but have no validity in modern English. Ending a sentence with a preposition is entirely proper and, in fact, is preferred if it results in a clear, natural-sounding sentence:

> It was the highest mortgage rate we had ever heard of.
> Jones is someone worth talking to.

The alternatives are tongue twisters: "It was the highest mortgage rate of which we had ever heard." "Jones is someone with whom it is worthwhile to talk."

On the other hand, the end of a sentence is an emphatic position. Rephrase a sentence if doing so forces a key word to the end.

> This law is difficult to comply with.
> Complying with this law is difficult.

shifts in person

When you write, you adopt a perspective. You can speak from your point of view or from your company's ("I" or "we"), you can address the reader ("you"), or you can write about one or more third parties ("he," "she," "it," "they"). These perspectives are identified as first person, second person, and third person. All three are acceptable. What is *not* acceptable, however, is shifting perspective in a single sentence, or a series of sentences.

Some shifts in person are obvious:

> If an employee works hard, you may be promoted.

The sentence should be consistent, either all in third person or all in second person:

> If an employee works hard, he or she may be promoted.   OR
> If you work hard, you may be promoted.

In longer passages, shifts in person often go unnoticed:

> Although auditors do not purposely investigate records for fraud, they should be aware of the possibility of fraud. If you suspect fraud, notify a senior auditor immediately.

In this passage the writer shifts from the third person ("the auditors" and "they") to second person ("you"). The second sentence should be revised to be consistent with the first ("If auditors suspect fraud, they should notify a senior auditor immediately.") or the entire passage should be rewritten in the second person:

> Although you will not purposely investigate records for fraud, you should be aware of its possibility. If you suspect fraud, notify a senior auditor immediately.

since, to mean because

Using *since* with the meaning of *because* is acceptable unless using *since* results in ambiguity. The meaning of this sentence is clear:

> Since I'll be away, I'd like to reschedule the meeting.

But two interpretations of the following sentence are possible:

> Since you resigned, the office has fallen apart.

It can mean (1) "Because you resigned, the office has fallen apart" or (2) "During the time you have been gone, the office has fallen apart."

In using *since,* simply make sure that your meaning is unambiguous.

split infinitive

Use of the split infinitive (putting a word between *to* and the verb, as in "to *fully* appreciate," or "to *casually* remark") is much debated in some offices. It is, however, no longer debated among language experts.

Over sixty years ago, in the first edition of *A Dictionary of Modern English Usage,* H. W. Fowler divided the English-speaking world into five groups: "(1) those who neither know nor care what a split infinitive is; (2) those who do not know, but care very much; (3) those who know and condemn; (4) those who know and approve; and (5) those who know and distinguish." In the ensuing six decades, the vast majority of authorities have echoed the words of Fowler, "We will split infinitives sooner than be ambiguous or artificial."

Awkward: *Really* to understand the problem, you should visit the work site.

Natural: To *really* understand the problem, you should visit the work site.

Awkward: Employees want *better* to understand the implications of the plan.

Natural: Employees want to *better* understand the implications of the plan.

Fowler gives the example of a sentence that is made ambiguous when an infinitive is not split: "Our object is *further* to cement trade relations." In this case the reader is "doubtful whether an additional 'object' or additional 'cementing' is the point." Fowler shows how splitting the infinitive eliminates the ambiguity: "Our object is to *further* cement trade relations."

The vast majority of sentences sound natural without splitting the infinitive: "The supervisor asked employees to report *immediately* any unsafe conditions." There is, in fact, no great merit in splitting an infinitive unless splitting it makes a sentence clearer or more natural sounding.

subject/verb agreement

The grammatical requirement that subjects and verbs agree (that is, both must be plural or both singular) is usually easy to meet. But here are a few troublesome situations:

Intervening Phrase. Frequently a phrase falls between the subject and verb:

> The duties of a manager *(include/includes)* making sure the staff is content. INCLUDE is correct. (Duties . . . include.)
> The length of my letters *(vary/varies)*. VARIES is correct. (Length . . . varies.)

Ignore prepositional phrases coming after the subject when deciding which verb form to use. (The prepositions most likely to create confusion are *of, from, for, in, on, to.*) To prevent being distracted by them, you may wish to bracket prepositional phrases (either mentally or physically) so that they do not obscure the structure of the sentence.

> None [of the vice-presidents] *has* offered any advice.
> A group [of angry stockholders] is expected to attend the annual meeting.

Subjects Containing "Or." Occasionally two subjects (one singular and one plural) may be separated by "or":

> Either the chairperson or the committee members *(has/have)* to work fast if the deadline is to be met.

When one part of the subject is singular and one part plural, the verb agrees with the part closer to it. Thus, in the example above *have* is correct. It follows, of course, that if the order within the subject is reversed, the verb must be changed:

> Either the committee members or the chairperson *has* to work fast if the deadline is to be met.

Subjects That Follow the Verb. Sometimes the verb appears before the subject:

> After the holidays *(come/comes)* the slump in sales.

Since the delayed subject is *slump,* the verb should be singular— *comes.* In the following sentence, the subject is plural. So too is the verb.

> Enclosed *are* the catalogue and the price list.

Subjects That Look Plural. Finally, some subjects are plural in form but singular in meaning:

> A million dollars *was* too much for that equipment.
> Three hours *is* too long to wait.

that

That may be omitted in a sentence, as long as its meaning is clear:

> Jean knows [that] she has to work hard to be promoted.
> She said [that] she would be willing to work overtime.

But *that* should be retained when its deletion causes misreading, as in the following:

> Chris showed us the report was accurate.
> Ezra said in June he was going on vacation.

In the first instance, Chris didn't show us the report. Rather,

> Chris showed us *that* the report was accurate.

In the second sentence, the meaning is ambiguous. Putting *that* in one of two places clarifies the meaning:

Ezra said *that* in June he was going on vacation.
Ezra said in June *that* he was going on vacation.

That may also be used if it improves the rhythm of a sentence:

> I think *that* I shall never see
> A poem lovely as a tree.

that, which

In deciding whether to use *that* or *which* in a sentence, you must first determine if the group of words introduced by *that* or *which* is essential to the meaning of the sentence or simply supplies extra information.

Compare these two sentences:

The house that Jack built is for sale.
The large brown Victorian house, which Jack built, is for sale.

In the first sentence above, the clause "that Jack built" is essential to the meaning of the sentence for it identifies the house. In the second sentence, the clause "which Jack built" gives additional information about the house, but does not identify it.

When the information is essential to the sentence, *that* is ordinarily used. No commas are necessary. When the information is supplementary or additional, *which* is used. Commas are necessary.

Compare the two pairs of sentences below noticing how *that* and *which* have been used. Notice, too, where commas have been used.

The policy that covers sick leave has been broadened.
Policy 32A, which covers sick leave, has been broadened.

The company that merged with Rego Industries is moving to St. Paul. Flint Inc., which merged with Rego Industries, is moving to St. Paul.

who, whom

The rules regarding *who* and *whom* are not applied as strictly as they once were. Some authorities accept *who* whenever it comes at the beginning of a sentence. Thus, "Who did you see?" is considered an alternative to "Whom did you see?" "Who did he ask for?" is acceptable, though "For whom did he ask?" would be preferred by the purist.

Most of us use *whom* quite naturally when it follows a preposition: "Jim is the person *to whom* the telegram was sent." "Beth is the boss *for whom* I have the most respect." But because using "whom" sometimes sounds heavy or wordy, rephrasing the sentence is often preferable: "The telegram was sent to Jim." "Beth is the boss I most respect."

Sometimes you can't avoid using *who* or *whom.* In these cases you will use *who* or *whom* correctly if you play with the sentence a bit and try substituting *he* or *him* for the troublesome *who* or *whom.* Simply replace the questionable *who(m),* first with *he* and then with *him.* If *he* fits, use *who;* if *him* fits, use *whom.* Here's how it works:

Questionable sentence:
Tell me *who/whom* will get the job.

Substitutions:
(1) *he* will get the job. (correct)
(2) *him* will get the job. (incorrect)
Solution: Tell me *who* will get the job.

It is often necessary to reverse the word order to use the substitution test.

Questionable sentence:
I don't know *who/whom* I should invite.

Substitutions:
  (1) I should invite *he*. (incorrect)
  (2) I should invite *him*. (correct)
Solution: I don't know *whom* I should invite.

Alas, not all sentences are quite as easy as those examples:

Questionable sentence:
  Give the message to *whoever/whomever* answers the phone.
Substitutions:
  (1) *he* answers the phone. (correct)
  (2) *him* answers the phone. (incorrect)
Solution: Give the message to *whoever* answers the phone.

The trick here is to recognize that *whoever* goes with "answers the phone," *not* with "Give the message to."

Someday the distinction between *who* and *whom* may disappear completely. Who knows?

Punctuation Review

Punctuation marks allow you to indicate in a written passage the pauses, inflections, and stopping places of the spoken language. Your speech pattern, your tone of voice, your self-interruptions or asides—all can come across through the various punctuation marks you use.

The signal system is standard, yet in a few cases there is some room for individual preference. Some writers always insert a comma before *and* in the final item in a series. Others omit the final comma. Some writers use dashes liberally. Others use a less emphatic comma or colon. The system is not totally arbitrary, however. Each mark does serve a specific purpose. If you use the marks properly, your readers will move along, pause, and stop just where you want them to. Moreover, your meaning will sometimes be clearer.

Punctuation is not difficult to learn. Besides reviewing the rules, you may find it helpful to observe how punctuation marks are used in major newspapers and magazines. Studying the punctuation in only one paragraph each day can help you master the marks.

The following review presents the major rules that apply to business writing.

apostrophe

The apostrophe has two uses:

- To indicate omission of a letter or number:

  don't   we'll   o'clock   the class of '75

- To indicate possession:

  If the possessive word is singular, add an apostrophe and *s*:

  the company's goals   Smith's salary   James's work load

(If adding a second *s* makes pronunciation difficult, add only the apostrophe: Moses' commandments.)

If the possessive word is plural and ends in *s,* add just an apostrophe:

> the companies' reports   the accountants' manuals
> the Joneses' mansion   three months' delay

If the possessive word is plural and does not end in *s,* add an apostrophe and *s:*

> the foremen's complaints   the children's voices

It's easy to get confused. Try flipping the words around, using the word *of,* when you are unsure of yourself. If the *s* is not on the word, add an apostrophe and *s*. If the *s* is already on the word, simply add an apostrophe:

the goals of the company = the company's goals
the reports of the companies = the companies' reports

Do not use the apostrophe with pronouns that are already possessive *(his, hers, its, ours, yours, theirs,* and *whose)*:

The book was *hers.*
The company and *its* subsidiary are located in the same building.

Note: The apostrophe was once used to form plurals of numbers and letters (*1970's, P's* and *Q's*). The use has fallen away. No apostrophe is required (*1970s, Ps* and *Qs*) unless adding just the *s* forms a word (*As, Us*). In that case, do use an apostrophe and *s* (*A's, U's*).

colon

Besides its conventional use after the salutation in a formal business letter, the colon has two other primary uses:

- To introduce a list or a series of ideas:

  The following officers attended the meeting: Lee Christie, Maria Rodriguez, Nick Lavdas.

  Please bring these items to the booth: the chart showing sales and earnings for five years, copies of the annual report, and new-product questionnaires.

The colon *is not* necessary in the following sentence:

  The new centers will be in: Phoenix, Dallas, and St. Louis.

- To link two closely related ideas or sentences. The information after the colon explains the preceding information:

  He had but one fear: losing his job.
  The drug will have two effects: It will eliminate itchiness and it will reduce swelling.

Note: A complete sentence should precede the colon. A phrase or a complete sentence may follow the colon. Capitalize the first word of the sentence following the colon. If a phrase follows the colon, no capital is necessary.

comma

The comma is the most used punctuation mark. There are many rules and many exceptions to the rules. Use the comma in the following ways:

- To separate parts of dates and place names:

  April 5, 1988   Portland, Maine   London, England

A comma follows the date and place name when they appear in sentences—unless they end a sentence.

  On April 5, 1988, Carl Winters announced plans for a new plant in Portland, Maine, the company's first plant in the Northeast.

When only the month and the year are used, no commas are required:

  In March 1988 their plant was damaged by fire.

Note: Because the U.S. Postal Service now uses an Optical Character Reader to sort mail, it asks that no comma be used between the city and state on envelopes or mailing labels that are typed (TUCSON AZ 85710). They also ask that you use no other punctuation, a uniform left margin, and all capital letters. Call your local post office to obtain Publication 25, "A Guide to Business Mail Preparation."

- To separate names from titles or degrees that follow:

  Paul R. Payton, Jr.
  Maria Whitcomb, M.D.
  Anthony Cabot, Esq.

In sentences, a comma is required after the title or degree:

  Paul R. Payton, Jr., married Maria Whitcomb, M.D., last week.

- To separate items in a series:

  a. The trainees were bright, hardworking, and enthusiastic.
  b. The job required them to work long hours, to travel for days at a time, and to bring in a stipulated amount of business monthly.

Using the comma before the final *and* is recommended. It can never be wrong and sometimes it prevents ambiguity. If beach umbrellas come in "red, white and blue" you may not be sure if you have two or three choices of color *(red, white and blue* OR *red, white, blue)*.

When several descriptive words precede one noun, commas may be unnecessary:

    c.   The streamlined inventory system allowed them to check the availability of a product within minutes.

An easy way to tell whether a comma is necessary is to substitute the word *and* for the comma. If *and* sounds all right between the words, use the comma. In sentence (a) above, you can say "bright, and hardworking, and enthusiastic"; thus, a comma can be used instead of the word *and,* or in addition to it for the final item. In sentence (c), *and* does not fit between the words. You do not mean "streamlined and inventory"; thus no comma is used.

- To separate two complete sentences joined by *and, but, nor, or, for, yet, so* (the comma comes *before* these joining words):

  The clerks wanted to be unionized, and they made that want known to management.
  Management refused to comment publicly, but they argued at length privately.

  If the two sentences are very short, no comma is needed:

  They fought hard but they did not win.

- To separate *yes, no,* and words of direct address from the rest of the sentence:

  Yes, they did approve the plan.
  Mike, let me know if you want to work with us.

- To separate an introductory phrase or clause from the main part of the sentence:

  After the prototype was produced, it was tested.
  Pleased with the results, management recommended that production begin immediately.

Because no marketing budget had been allocated, sales were slow
initially.

If the introductory expression is short, the comma is sometimes
omitted:

After March we will be using the new system.

- To separate contrasting ideas:

Kate said $1.5 million, not $1.8 million, was approved.
It was to be spent for research, not development.

- To enclose interrupting, nonessential, or parenthetical information:

Ben had, of course, remembered to book reservations.
The club, usually busy, was nearly empty that day.

- To set off appositives, that is, a word or words that identify or
describe a preceding word:

Marcia Campbell, our treasurer, will be addressing the group.
The Omni Group, a consortium of international investors, will publish
the newsletter.

dash

The dash is an emphatic punctuation mark. It indicates a break or
shift in thought. The dash signals a pause greater than that signaled by the comma or colon and less than that signaled by parentheses.

The dash can be used to introduce an expression that completes
the first idea or expresses an afterthought:

The company has but one goal—to become profitable.
Sam said we'd all get raises—maybe next year or the year after that.

Pairs of dashes can be used in the middle of a sentence to interject
a quick interrupting thought or to convey clarifying information:

Herbal Logs—to be introduced next fall—will be a popular item for Christmas gifts.

Two laws—those pertaining to IRAs—came up for discussion.

Pairs of dashes are also used to set off parenthetical elements that contain internal commas:

He said he hoped—but would, of course, not promise—that bonus checks would be given out today.

exclamation point

The exclamation point may be used after emphatic statements and commands. It should not be used, however, as a substitute for a more emphatic word or phrase. Overuse of the exclamation point may make writing seem overly casual or adolescent.

An exclamation point should be used here:

Congratulations! I've just heard about your promotion.

But this sentence should be revised:

Sales for the first quarter increased substantially!
Sales for the first quarter soared by 56%.

hyphen

The most common use of the hyphen is to divide a word at the end of a line. Such a hyphen must come between syllables. The hyphen has four other uses:

• To attach some prefixes and suffixes:

prefixes: ex-, quasi-, half-, quarter-, self- (self-interest)
suffixes: -elect, -odd (twenty-odd dollars)

Many words that were once hyphenated are now written without the hyphen:

cooperative   semicolon   reinforce

However, if the root word is capitalized, the hyphen is still required:

un-American   anti-Soviet   post-Vietnam

To be sure of any specific word, consult your dictionary.

- To join compound words:

eighty-six   cover-up   great-grandmother

The dictionary also shows hyphenated compound words.

- To connect two or more words that have a single meaning:

long-term debt   out-of-date equipment
across-the-board raises   state-of-the-art technology

When the words hyphenated in the examples above, or others, are used after the noun, no hyphens are used:

Raises were given across the board.

- To prevent misreading:

a dirty-book salesman   a dirty book-salesman

period

The period is used in the following ways:

- After statements, requests, or indirect questions:

The shipment is to arrive today.
Please let me know as soon as it gets here.
Would you also tell Beverly when it's here.
She has asked about it for days.

- After some abbreviations:

A.M.	P.M.	B.A.	M.A.	Ph.D.	Ms.	Mrs.
Mr.	M.D.	Co.	Inc.	U.S.A.	U.K.	F.O.B.

But many abbreviations and acronyms are written without periods:

IRS, UNESCO, LIFO, YMCA, and so on. (See "Abbreviations" on page 121.)

question mark

Use a question mark after direct questions:

Did he get promoted?
What will his new title be? Director? Senior partner?

quotation marks

Quotation marks are used in the following ways:

- To enclose direct quotations:

The chairman said on more than one occasion, "Our company is not a candidate for takeover."

But not indirect quotations:

The chairman said that our company is not a takeover candidate.

- To enclose titles of essays, articles, television programs, and chapters or sections of longer works:

"Cable Today, Gone Tomorrow," written by my partner, appeared on the front page of the business section.

- To denote coined words or words used in a special sense:

The "bikeathon" will be sponsored next Sunday.
Technical analysts on Wall Street are sometimes referred to as "gnomes."

Other Punctuation Marks with Quotation Marks. The period and the comma are always placed inside the final quotation mark. The colon and semicolon are placed after the final mark:

> The differences in storage methods are described in the second section of the report, "Safe Storage."
> Temporary dumps, or "hold-dumps," store waste for up to three months.
> Long-term dumps are referred to as "perm-dumps"; however, they are not truly permanent.

When a question mark is used with quotation marks, it may fall inside or outside the final quotation mark. If the quoted material is itself a question, the question mark is placed inside the quotation marks. If the whole sentence is a question, the question mark is placed outside the quotation marks.

> He asked, "Would you consider reducing your fee?"
> Did you tell him "absolutely not"?

semicolon

The semicolon has two uses:

- To connect two sentences that are closely related:

> We have no alternative; we must act now.
> Raises are justified; productivity has risen.
> Profits are down; however, the future of the company is secure.

The third sentence above illustrates the most common use of the semicolon—that is, when the second complete sentence begins with a word like *however, therefore, thus, consequently, furthermore.* (For a fuller discussion of conjunctive adverbs, see "Comma Splice" on page 123 of the glossary.)

- To connect elements in a series when one or more elements contain commas:

Please send your comments to one of these committee members: Pat Warner, director; Nilda Falcon, bureau chief; or Wallace Christiansen, project officer.

The president sought opinions on her plan from the vice-president, who supported it; the treasurer, who opposed it; and a consultant, who recommended further study.

Afterword

Reading Can Help Your Writing

If you read a lot, you will develop a sense for the language and for the written word. You will store away, quite unconsciously, patterns, phrases, and rhythms that will help you write better.

Read books, magazines, and newspapers, as well as business correspondence. But read critically. Not every piece of writing is well written. After you have finished reading a memo, letter, or report—or anything, for that matter—ask yourself if it was clear and easy to read. If it was, take a moment to analyze how it was written. If it was not, analyze where the writer went wrong. Try to learn from his or her mistakes.

Consult reference books and other books about writing. Skim the books and become familiar with them in your spare time. Then when you're having trouble writing, you'll know which expert to turn to.

The following books are among my favorites:

Reference Books

Copperud, Roy L. *American Style and Usage: The Consensus.* New York: Van Nostrand Reinhold Company, 1980.

This book is really eight books in one. It compares the opinions of eight authorities on specific points of usage.

Morris, William, ed. *The American Heritage Dictionary of the English Language.* Boston: Houghton Mifflin Company, 1981.
What a wonderful dictionary! It takes the language seriously. Its usage experts are among the most respected guardians of the language. Its definitions are clear.

Oliu, Walter E., Charles T. Brusaw, and Gerald J. Alred. *The Business Writer's Handbook,* 3rd ed. New York: St. Martin's Press, 1987.
If you need a quick answer to a question concerning grammar, usage, or business writing in general, this book will provide it. It is clear and up-to-date.

Books about Writing

Ewing, David, *Writing for Results,* 2nd ed. New York: John Wiley & Sons, 1979.
Ewing, formerly executive editor of *Harvard Business Review,* discusses writing with his readers. His style is relaxed; his examples are often witty.

Holcombe, Marya W., and Judith K. Stein. *Writing for Decision Makers,* 2nd ed. New York: Van Nostrand Reinhold Company, 1987.
This book describes the decisions a writer must make when writing. It offers sound advice.

Munter, Mary. *Guide to Managerial Communication,* 2nd ed. Englewood Cliffs, N.J.: Prentice-Hall, Inc., 1987.
Although this book provides few examples, it nicely summarizes techniques you can use in planning and preparing written and oral presentations.

Strunk, William Jr., and E. B. White. *The Elements of Style,* 3rd ed. New York: Macmillan Publishing Co., Inc., 1979.
If you enjoy reading about writing, you must read this classic. It is sophisticated and clever.

Weiss, Edmond H. *The Writing System for Engineers and Scientists.* Englewood Cliffs, N.J.: Prentice-Hall, 1982.

Though the book's title targets specific readers, its solid advice can help everyone in business.

Williams, Joseph M. *Style: Ten Lessons in Clarity and Grace,* 2nd ed. Glenville, Ill.: Scott, Foresman and Company, 1985.
If you are truly interested in achieving a simple and clear style, you will benefit from this book. Williams assumes his reader has an understanding of grammar. Exercises appear after each chapter; answers are provided.

Zinsser, William. *On Writing Well,* 3rd ed. New York: Harper & Row, 1988.
While Zinsser does not deal specifically with business writing, he does help his readers understand what "writing well" is all about. The book is a delight.

Index